a SAVOR THE SOUTH® *cookbook*

Sunday Dinner

SAVOR THE SOUTH® *cookbooks*

Sunday Dinner, by Bridgette A. Lacy (2015)
Crabs and Oysters, by Bill Smith (2015)
Beans and Field Peas, by Sandra A. Gutierrez (2015)
Gumbo, by Dale Curry (2015)
Shrimp, by Jay Pierce (2015)
Catfish, by Paul and Angela Knipple (2015)
Sweet Potatoes, by April McGreger (2014)
Southern Holidays, by Debbie Moose (2014)
Okra, by Virginia Willis (2014)
Pickles and Preserves, by Andrea Weigl (2014)
Bourbon, by Kathleen Purvis (2013)
Biscuits, by Belinda Ellis (2013)
Tomatoes, by Miriam Rubin (2013)
Peaches, by Kelly Alexander (2013)
Pecans, by Kathleen Purvis (2012)
Buttermilk, by Debbie Moose (2012)

a SAVOR THE SOUTH® *cookbook*

Sunday Dinner

BRIDGETTE A. LACY

The University of North Carolina Press CHAPEL HILL

The paper in this book meets the guidelines for permanence and durability of
the Committee on Production Guidelines for Book Longevity of the Council on
Library Resources. The University of North Carolina Press has been a member
of the Green Press Initiative since 2003.

Jacket photograph by Lisa Tutman-Oglesby

Library of Congress Cataloging-in-Publication Data
Lacy, Bridgette A.
Sunday dinner / Bridgette A. Lacy.—1st [edition].
pages cm.—(Savor the South cookbooks)
Includes bibliographical references and index.
ISBN 978-1-4696-2245-3 (cloth : alk. paper)—ISBN 978-1-4696-2246-0 (ebook)
1. Dinners and dining. 2. Cooking, American—Southern style. I. Title.
TX737.L27 2015   641.5′4—dc23
2015006181

The recipes for Original Baker's German's Sweet Chocolate Cake and Coconut-
Pecan Filling and Frosting are reprinted here courtesy of Kraft Foods.

*In loving memory of my grandparents,
the late Marie and James R. Moore Jr., for some of
the best Sunday dinners and moments of my life.
Thank you, Papa, for teaching me the first bite is
with the eye and the beauty of a meal well-served.
Thank you, Grandma, for your love, grace, and
guidance in the kitchen and in life.*

*And for my mother, Esther Lacy Claxton,
for continuing the fine tradition.*

Contents

a SAVOR THE SOUTH® *cookbook*

Sunday Dinner

Introduction

FOOD AS LOVE

My earliest food memories are of sitting on my grand-father's lap, cutting my teeth on bacon at my grand-parents' home in Lynchburg, Virginia. I was his first grandchild, and he called me his sugar girl. I named him Papa. James Russell Moore Jr. was one of the best cooks I have ever known. He knew how to prepare what he called "a good something to eat," especially on the Sabbath.

He grew lots of fruits and vegetables. His cantaloupes were so sweet, they tasted like he had poured sugar in the ground. He bought his flour for making yeast rolls and cakes from a bakery. His pantry was organized with canned goods clearly labeled and cooking gadgets and utensils neatly stacked in their boxes. On Saturday and Sunday afternoons, there was a flurry of activity in the kitchen. And I had a seat at the table.

Preparing the Sunday meal was a family affair at my grand-parents' home. I learned to peel potatoes, snap the ends off string beans, and rinse tomatoes, squash, and other produce from Papa's backyard garden. My mother chopped celery, sliced onions, or washed dishes. Grandma shaped the yeast rolls and fried the chicken. Aunt Barbara Anne set the dining room table for the big meal.

As a young girl, on warm summer days, I experienced Sunday dinner sitting down with my grandparents, parents, aunts and uncles, siblings, and cousins to a meal of fried chicken, potato salad, green beans, and yeast rolls. On cold winter afternoons, Sunday dinner meant generous portions of perfectly seasoned pot roast with mashed potatoes and carrots. The meals were always made with the freshest seasonal produce—often from Papa's gar-den or a farmers' market—along with the nicer cuts of meats and homemade desserts, including coconut pies and what Papa called his Nilla Wafer Brown Pound Cake.

Unlike weekdays, Sunday was a time when everyone was expected to gather around the table at the same time. Visiting relatives such as Papa's sister, my great-aunt Ernestine, who lived in New York, and close friends were invited to share a seat at the table on Sundays more than any other day. Or maybe my mother's brother, Uncle Moco, who lived a few houses up the street, and his family, would be at the table. Sometimes my grandmother's sister, Aunt Mary Pullen, and her husband, Uncle Weldon, would join us.

The meal was never rushed, and all lingered at the table for second helpings. There was a lot of "please" and "thank you" heard around the table, as well as "yes, sir" and "no, ma'am."

After dinner, while some of us cleared the table, others retreated to the living room or the front or back porch, depending on the weather.

Sunday dinner was the artistic expression of my grandfather's love for his family, and it was a masterpiece. He worked at the foundry molding pipe during the week, but on the weekends, those hands produced the most delicate pies, cakes, and hearty entrées.

My grandfather came from a large family of ten children. He was born in 1918 to James and Ernestine Moore. His family owned a fifty-five-acre farm in Madison Heights, Virginia, with a chicken coop, a hog pen, and a shelter for a milking cow, surrounded by rows of corn, tomatoes, squash, and green beans for the dinner table.

Papa met my grandmother when she taught his siblings in a one-room schoolhouse. Marie Moorman stood 5-feet-10-inches tall, recited poetry beautifully, and exhibited an air of sophistication. On occasion, his family invited her to dinner. Papa courted grandma by playing "Ain't She Sweet" on his ukulele as they walked along the bank of the James River. Grandma often recalled that she liked him in part because he wasn't stingy. Another suitor, she said, bought her a soda, only to drink half before she took the first sip. I cherished the telling of that story during those luxurious hours on Sunday afternoons.

To have the privilege of putting your feet under Papa's square dining room table was downright spiritual.

For some, Sunday dinner represents a snapshot of that wonderful time and place where families gathered and recharged, and for others, it may be the start of a ritual they've only heard about through older family members. For all, it will be a reminder to carve out that sacred space in life to cherish family and friends and celebrate the big and small moments. Sunday dinner helped shape me as a person. It was during those meals that I expressed my dream of becoming a writer. It was during those meals that I bonded with country cousins, eccentric aunts and uncles, and cherished grandparents. It was during those meals that I learned the rich history of my proud family. We laughed, loved, and ate. We left the table with our hearts and bellies full.

Sunday still commands a certain type of reverence. Many southerners still feel the need to get in the kitchen and deliver a feast for those closest to them. It often starts with carefully selecting fresh produce from the farmers' market on Saturday, then rising early on Sunday morning to marinate and season meats or shape yeast rolls needing to rise by dinnertime.

My grandparents are gone now, but most Sunday afternoons, I return to that table where my love for that sacred meal first started. It's uncanny how many times my mother and I are eating the same dishes on Sunday afternoon even though we are separated by 263 miles and we haven't discussed the meal ahead of time.

Sunday dinner, especially in the South, is more than a meal—it's a state of mind. It's about taking the time to be with the people who matter to you. During the week, we often are rushing—to get home, to get to a meeting, or to get to a child's after-school activity. On Sunday, we can slow down, relax, and savor the food and relationships that will nourish us for the rest of the week.

Today, there are fewer large family clans. Children have moved far away from parents and grandparents. Uncles and cousins no longer live within walking distance. Many of us who grew up eating Sunday dinner surrounded by family now eat dinner alone. For others, Sunday dinner has become an afternoon at the local all-you-can-eat buffet, eating among tables of strangers.

But the lure of Sunday dinner has never left. And so as a single woman, I have often sought out friends and colleagues to join my culinary communion especially on Sundays.

Like many Americans especially during the week, I eat dinner alone. Sometimes I scarf down my food while watching television in my bedroom, between appointments while running errands in the car, or standing at the kitchen counter. I have lots of company. More than 50 percent of U.S. residents are single. About 33 percent of all households have just one resident.

Even people who live with spouses and children often fall into this habit of dining solo. Few folks walk into a home filled with the sweet scent of a home-cooked meal. Families are more likely to grab a slice of pizza from the delivery box, a microwaved entrée, or a salad. These quick bites of mindless food normally don't seem worthy of sitting at the table or even pulling out dinnerware.

It's no wonder I savor the meals I share with others. Food tastes better when you are surrounded by people who appreciate the preparation of a home-cooked meal. There's a delight that comes from the face of someone who understands the work you put into making a dish delicious. Companionship is the seasoning, the secret ingredient that factors into the recipe. I learned that as a child at the dining room table in my maternal grandparents' house during Sunday dinner. That's why I love to invite people over for that feast of a meal or go to someone else's home on Sundays. I mourn those days when there was a house full of people who I loved at the table. I have been trying to reproduce the same warm and loving experience at my own home most of my life. My grandparents set the bar high.

The Sabbath and Dinner

The rhythm of Sunday was unique in the South, the Bible Belt. The country's first blue laws, restricting activities or sales of goods on Sunday to accommodate the Christian Sabbath, were enacted in Virginia. The first blue law in the American colonies was enacted in Virginia in 1617. It required church attendance and authorized the militia to force colonists to attend church services. Sunday was a day of rest, not for commerce.

In my grandparents' home, Sunday started with my grandmother singing "What a Friend We Have in Jesus" as she fried eggs and bacon on the gas stove. Marie Moore sang it as if it were testimony to the trials and tribulations of a woman who had already lost two siblings before I was born. She sang like the determined woman who attended school for ten summers to complete her degree from Virginia State College in Petersburg. My siblings and I were often sent to Sunday school and joined the adults on the pew for Sunday service at Diamond Hill Baptist Church, the same church my great-grandparents had attended.

Family members—teachers and blue-collar workers—didn't work that day. That left more leisure time to make dishes that were more elaborate and labor-intensive. Sunday dinner had more prestige. The telephone seldom rang; everyone knew it was dinnertime.

Like many family cooks across America, after church, grandma heated up vegetables cooked earlier, fried the chicken, and placed the rolls in the oven. Judging by the increased number of cars parked on the street, I figured that same ritual was happening throughout the neighborhood.

For my family, the Sabbath was Sunday, but many religions and cultures choose another day to celebrate faith, family, and food. These families also open their homes to invited guests from their places of worship, communities, and neighborhoods.

Many Jewish families gather around the table on Friday night, light two Sabbath candles, and break challah with family and neighbors and friends as they prepare for Saturday service. Italian families enjoy their holy feast of an antipasto platter, bruschetta, and homemade pastas and gravy, a rich tomato-based sauce with numerous cuts of meat on the Sabbath. In South Africa, families savor their sweet potatoes, pumpkin, and roasted meats for their lunch gathering on their day of rest. Greeks gather around the table for an afternoon meal of lamb and pastitsio, a Greek lasagna, and spanakopita. The food varies, but it's the meal that brings everyone together.

Passed Down

My mother maintained the tradition of the Sunday meal at our home in Washington, D.C. Her table, too, was beautiful and elaborate, but it was a smaller round table, with fewer people and fewer dishes. My father's palate influenced this table; he favored scalloped potatoes, short ribs of beef, and butternut squash. Of course, Papa's recipes also informed this dinner. My mother had mastered the Papa's Nilla Wafer Brown Pound Cake and often made the dessert, especially when two church ladies would visit. Their red lipstick stained the glasses they drank from during the meal.

During my college years, I often brought classmates home for dinner. We boarded the bus from Howard University's campus to ride downtown and catch the Red Line subway to my parent's home. My mother, like her daddy, made a big pot of greens and fried chicken, often referred to by church folks as the gospel bird because attending the Sunday service and eating fried chicken for supper go hand in hand.

I, too, loved eating at my mother's table, but at my grandparent's house, I was the sugar girl, the oldest grandchild; I was special. I didn't realize then that the feeling of safety and comfort they brought me would serve me all of my life.

What my elders intrinsically knew was that Sunday dinner was not just about the present and who gathered on that day, nor did it simply echo the past and all that had always been. Our shared Sunday dinners were about my future. Those times would mold who I would become as a person, as an adult.

Scholars have reached the same conclusion. According to the Family Dinner Project, a grassroots movement of food, fun, and conversation, over the past fifteen years, research has shown that sharing a family meal is good for the spirit, brain, and health of all family members.

Recent studies link regular family meals with the kinds of behaviors that parents want for their children: higher grade-point averages, resilience, and self-esteem. Additionally, family meals are linked to lower rates of substance abuse, teen pregnancy, eating disorders, and depression. Researchers believe in the power of family dinners to nourish ethical thinking.

According to a 2012 study from Columbia University's National Center on Addiction and Substance Abuse, teenagers who eat dinner with their parents are less likely to participate in risky behavior, including smoking, drug use, and drinking alcohol. "This year's study again demonstrates that the magic that happens at family dinners isn't the food on the table, but the conversations and family engagement around the table," wrote Joseph A. Califano Jr., founder and chairman emeritus of CASAColumbia.

William Doherty, a professor of family social science at the University of Minnesota, had this advice for parents and caregivers who have given up on family dinners: "Start on a Sunday night."

For our family, Sunday dinner often started with spending personal time with our grandparents, sometimes in the garden picking green beans or shucking corn. My cousin Jeff shared with me how when Papa took him to the grocery store, he often held his hand. Jeff's father had died when Jeff was a toddler, so that really meant a lot to him.

We also left with confidence in ourselves that we could overcome frustration in school, at the job, or in life. As the fictional matriarch of the movie *Soul Food* expressed, "One finger won't make an impact, but you ball all those fingers into a fist, and you can strike a mighty blow. Now, this family has got to be that fist."

Simple Beauty

Sunday dinner was not just a meal on the plate; it was a palate of rich colors and textures. In my family, Sunday dinner meant that the table was set with ironed linen. The good china and the silver sat alongside the gold- and silver-colored aluminum tumblers that kept the sweet tea nice and cold. The fried chicken and butter beans were seasoned to perfection. I can still recall Papa's potato salad. He would trim the potato salad with sliced eggs going around the bowl and then sprinkle the dish with paprika. It was a thing of beauty. He taught me the first bite is with the eye. Anything you needed was already on the table. When you sat down, you didn't get up until there was no more room for another tasty morsel. Young and old folks sampled a little of everything. It was a day of joy, harmony, and satisfaction.

As an African American woman, I experienced Sunday dinner as a time when the matriarch and patriarch of the family took their rightful place at the head of the table to bless the food and all that coming together for a meal symbolized. Grandparents were revered for their cooking skills, as well as their wisdom. Problems disappeared during those cherished hours.

Literary Meals

Characters real and fictional have been born at the table. Before Facebook and Twitter, family meals and porch-sitting were two of the great American pastimes and channels for conveying family news and gossip. Someone might bring a potential mate to such a gathering, which could make for interesting corner conversations after Sunday dinner. My grandmother would also tell cautionary tales of family members who had made bad choices and whose lives were impacted by those decisions.

Not so unlike the fictional Mattie Rigsbee, the main character in North Carolina author Clyde Edgerton's *Walking Across Egypt*. The seventy-eight-year-old Mattie is spunky and determined. She tries to help Wesley Benfield, a wayward teenager and orphan, by feeding and loving him. Edgerton describes a scene that could take place anywhere in the South: "Soon after the church service, Mattie, in the kitchen, looked into her oven. The biscuits were about ready. Robert and Laurie, Robert's new girlfriend, sat at the table, sipping iced tea, ready to eat. . . . Robert, Laurie, and Wesley started passing food. Peas and corn, creamed potatoes, pork chops, a pickle plate, string beans, sliced tomatoes, biscuits."

North Carolina's Reynolds Price recalls in his memoir, *Clear Pictures: First Loves, First Guides*, the care his aunt Ida took in preparation of the big meal: "Nephews, cousins and in-laws would hear of our arrival and gather at meal times. It was no chore apparently for Ida to serve a bountiful seated Sunday dinner, the midday meal, to fifteen or more. And on Sunday evenings, she could invite the long porchful of guests to stay for supper, then rise and work her own loaves-and-fishes miracle with two dozen eggs, a few slices of ham, endless fresh tomatoes and the hundred rolls she'd laid out to rise on Saturday night."

During World War II, there was even a movie *Sunday Dinner for a Soldier*, in which a poor family in Florida saves money so it can invite a soldier over for Sunday dinner. The family doesn't realize that its request to invite the soldier never got mailed. On the day of the scheduled dinner, another soldier is brought to their home, and love soon blossoms between him and Tessa, the young woman who runs the home.

During the early 1990s, when I worked as a reporter for the *Indianapolis Star*, a group of my fellow journalists and I would gather once a month for Sunday dinner. We took turns hosting the meal at each other's homes. When they come to my house, I served dinner on a card table covered by a pressed cotton table cloth, along with cotton napkins and real china. Derrick Stokes, the only man in our group, would make the same dish every time—a pot of spaghetti. He made the meat sauce in a heavy pot he had stolen from his mother's kitchen when he left his native Philadelphia to start his career as a police reporter. He also brought her recipe. During the final moment of cooking the rich sauce, he would add baby shrimp.

Whenever I make my sauce like Derrick's, I'm transported back to those Indianapolis dinners.

When I first came to Raleigh two decades ago, my Sunday dinner family was re-created in the form of the African American Classics Book Club. We took turns hosting potluck get-togethers once a month. Often the host would supply standard Sunday dinner staples, including homemade macaroni and cheese, fried chicken, and pasta salads.

While we gathered to talk about books, we broke bread discussing the travails and triumphs of life as a black professional. This literary and culinary oasis buoyed our spirits beyond the dinner table.

On weekends when I didn't have book club, I drove three hours on the scenic U.S. Route 501 to Lynchburg, Virginia, the city of seven hills, to visit and, yes, eat dinner.

In her later years, grandma, like many Americans, was left to eat alone most evenings because her children and grandchildren were grown and spread out across the country. During my weekend visits, we often sat at the red Formica table in her kitchen and ate smaller meals.

After grandma died and the house was sold, Uncle Moco, out of habit, would follow the walkway down the side of the house searching for those sounds and smells that had emanated from his parents' home for decades. Some of those emotions tugging at Uncle Moco still resonate in me.

Who wouldn't want that for the next generation—to feel a sense of place and belonging? In hindsight, what I realize in writing this cookbook is that families loved most passionately during these dinners.

I love *Sunday Dinner* being a part of the Savor the South collection. I wanted another generation to understand the joy of preparing the feast together as a family. I wanted another generation to learn how to make their favorite dishes by watching the matriarchs and patriarchs in their family. Even though my grandparents have left this earth, their memory remains in the creations on the plate.

Sunday dinner today could mean inviting other singles and small families to a potluck with everyone bringing a dish. It's a chance to connect with others and nourish the body and soul. The Sunday meal should remind us of our personal relationships with food and the people we love.

In recent years, I have often eaten dinner with writer Mary Miller and her family. Her children affectionately call me Aunt Poulet because I couldn't stop talking about the French rotisserie chicken I enjoyed during a three-month North Carolina Arts Council fellowship in the south of France. At Mary's house, almost every day is like a Sunday because she has four children and loves to cook from scratch. It's one of the ways she loves.

One day, I called Mary and mentioned that I had had a rough day. She came and picked me up for the afternoon. Another friend had joined us and her children. We sat at Mary's kitchen table painting pictures with her children as Mary prepared blistered green beans, sliced apples, small chunks of cheese, roasted tomatoes, and chicken spinach sausage over a bed of spinach.

Her husband, Bob Geolas, made a homemade dressing of mustard and olive oil. Mary served it with a crusty loaf of bread. She lit candles. Each of us at the table said what had been our "thorn" and "rose." Two of her children called Jim, the other guest, and me their rose. That whole afternoon lifted my spirit.

Those kinds of dinners are common at her home. Another evening, Mary cooked a wonderful lemon and ginger pork roast with roasted asparagus and fingerling potatoes. Afterward, we sat on the back porch and talked as we listened to the rain.

Not every family can produce that during a weekday, but it's worth a try on Sunday. It's a way of starting the week strong with your family.

One of the beauties of the traditional Sunday dinner was that you had a special meal and the foundation for meals to come. As Papa said, "If you cook a pot of greens on Sunday, you have the makings of a meal all week." You might have those leafy greens with fried chicken on a Sunday and meatloaf on a Tuesday. Leftover yeast rolls became the bread for a ham sandwich for the next day's lunch, and extra potato salad was saved for Tuesday night's dinner and served with another meat. The Sunday meal was so good that people welcomed the chance to taste it again during the coming week.

This cookbook features fifty recipes that are synonymous with Sunday dinner. They will delight and nourish readers. Some of the recipes are beloved classics; others are inspired by memories of Papa's table, and still others are favorites from family members and friends. The southern fare in the cookbook includes such classics as Sunday Yeast Rolls, Grandma's Fried Chicken, and Esther's Summer Potato Salad; Papa's recipes such as Big Jimmy's Coconut Pie and Papa's Nilla Wafer Brown Pound Cake; and collected favorites from family and friends, including Butternut Squash with Sage and Pumpkin Bread.

These recipes were chosen because they belong to our collected memories of growing up and sharing the feast of Sunday dinner. Family members knew they were going to spend some time preparing these meals that would become part of a family's history.

I offer a contemporary twist on some traditional dishes. For example, instead of preparing squash on the stove top, I offer Savory Stuffed Crookneck Squash, a delicious side dish made with bacon, cheese, and onions. For dessert, I suggest nixing the plain watermelon and creating my colorful and fresh-tasting Summer Fruit Salad. My grandparents cooked for a large family, but I often cook for just me. Most recipes yield six to eight servings, perfect for leftovers for smaller families.

Since families don't have as many hands in the kitchen as Papa did, I have included a couple of recipes that make strategic use of Crock-Pot also known as slow cookers. This popular appliance, known for simmering, will help get Sunday dinner on the table quickly. Slow cookers are great for tenderizing large pieces of meats as well as a convenient way to prepare pasta dishes. For example, I have a wonderful recipe for cooking macaroni and cheese in the crock pot while you might be in church.

Take advantage of butchered meats and precut vegetables to help get Sunday dinner on the table. If you don't have time to make a piecrust from scratch, buy one already made. There are no right and wrong ways to prepare the big dinner.

This cookbook is organized by courses: main dishes, sides, salads, breads, desserts, and drinks. No appetizer recipes are included because Sunday dinner needed no opening act. It was the feast of the week. Family members and guests reserved their appetites for the big meal.

Unlike weekday dinners, Sunday dinner, especially in the South, meant more meats, more sides, and more courses. It often meant homemade desserts instead of the store-bought treats often served during the week.

The recipes include headnotes that offer tips such as how to choose produce or pertinent food-related reminiscences. My aim for this book is to appeal both to people learning to cook and to those re-creating a family meal that holds sway in their memories. Many women and men may be returning to the kitchen after years of eating prepared food and takeout. Others, like the friends who have asked me, "How do you cook fresh green beans from scratch?" may be undertaking the cooking of a large meal for the first time.

Whether you're nostalgic or new to the tradition, you can create these mouth-watering meals with the help of family and friends and pacing yourself. Here are a few suggestions.

Tips for a Successful Sunday Dinner

* Prepare ahead of time for Sunday dinner. I like using the occasion as an excuse to perform some deep cleaning in common areas. Assign small housekeeping chores to yourself during the week, such as vacuuming the dining room floor or dusting the living room furniture.
* Schedule time Saturday morning to pick up produce from the farmers' market. This may be a good time to have some special alone time with grandparents or parents.
* If you are busy during the week, think about having a produce box delivered to your home.
* Set the table the evening before.
* Use real china and linen. What are you saving it for? Why not get the real stuff out of the cabinet for the people you love?
* Invite singles who often eat alone during the week for Sunday dinner. This will really make their week.
* Ask folks to bring one of their signature dishes to share. Men and women like to show off their culinary skills.
* Assign chores; people want to help out. Everyone can perform some task—fill the glasses with ice, set out napkins, or toss the salad. Enlist helpers to plate and serve each course.
* Serve dinner early in the afternoon between 2 P.M. and 4 P.M.
* Stick with a seasonal menu and have plenty of everything.
* Serve dishes at the right temperatures. Before you start dinner, map out the cooking times on each dish. Get the meat done and resting early. Work out how to keep food at the right temperature in advance.

- Stock the kitchen with plastic containers so folks can feel free to take leftovers home, or ask them to bring their own to-go containers.
- Start dinner with an empty dishwasher. This way, guests and family members can help by cleaning off the table and putting the dishes directly into the dishwasher instead of piling them up on the counter.
- Play word games or other games that get people talking, like Pictionary.
- Invite folks to take an after-dinner walk. This is a great way to build memories.

If you didn't grow up in a home with a Sunday dinner tradition, start your own. Here are a few tips:

- Incorporate rituals that are important to you and your family. For my mother and me, it's setting a pretty table with good china, fresh flowers, and cloth linen.
- Create your own family by asking coworkers, friends, and people from your social circles.
- Ask family members known for their cooking skills for recipes and tips. The next time you are visiting with one of those family members, spend some time in the kitchen watching what they do.
- Make dishes you've cooked before for large gatherings. If you're determined to impress guests with a new dish, give it a test run a few weeks in advance.
- Plan the menu strategically. I like serving one item that can be made ahead of time, one that goes in the oven, and one that I can cook on the stove top or reheat in the microwave.
- Have fun.

Remember, Sunday dinner is more than a meal, it's a state of mind. That means there should always be room for another set of hands in the kitchen, and room for another seat at the table.

Main Dishes

Sunday dinner in my family meant big meats and fried chicken. So this section includes recipes for Eye of Round Pot Roast with Baby Portabellas, Fragrant Sunday Chicken with Olives and Apricots, and Short Ribs. The savory smells from these meats made you want to come to the dinner table even before the meal was ready. These dishes yield yummy leftovers for lunch or additional dinners.

Grandma's Fried Chicken

On Sunday, my grandmother fried the chicken. As my grand-parents got older, Papa cooked most of the time. But after church, grandma stood tall at the right side of the stove, frying that crispy gospel bird in a skillet on the front burner. I've made a few changes to pack even more flavor to this Sunday dinner classic.

MAKES 6 SERVINGS

---

6 bone-in chicken breasts (or whatever parts your family likes)
Old Bay seasoning for seasoning the chicken,
   plus 2 tablespoons
2 cups all-purpose flour
2½ cups vegetable oil

Rinse the chicken breasts, season well with Old Bay, and place in a plastic bag. Refrigerate for at least 4 hours or overnight to marinate.

When ready to prepare the chicken for frying, bring it to room temperature, about 30 minutes. In a shallow container, combine the flour and Old Bay. Pat the chicken pieces dry and then dredge the chicken in the flour mixture until well coated.

Heat the oil in a large skillet until hot. "You want [the chicken] to start frying as soon as it hits the grease," my mother says. She sometimes tests the temperature of the oil with a small piece of bread. If it sizzles immediately, the oil is ready. Place the chicken in the skillet and fry, turning as it browns. Breasts, thighs, and legs will take 15–20 minutes, and wings about 10–15 minutes.

Drain the chicken on paper towels. Serve hot.

Mama's Meaty Crab Cakes

I request my mother's crab cakes almost every time I return to my childhood home. These meaty crab cakes flavored with Old Bay seasoning are far better than any I've had at a restaurant. They are crunchy on the outside from the cornmeal and moist on the inside. My mother serves them on Martin's potato rolls with potato salad. There will be no leftovers with these. In fact, get to the table fast. These won't last.

MAKES 8 SERVINGS

1 pound fresh jumbo lump or lump crabmeat

1 celery stalk, finely chopped

½ medium white onion, finely chopped

½ green bell pepper, finely chopped

2 tablespoons Hellmann's mayonnaise

1 teaspoon Old Bay seasoning, or more, to taste

⅓ cup Italian-seasoned bread crumbs

Cornmeal for dredging

2 cups vegetable oil (more or less, depending on the size of your skillet)

Place the crabmeat in a large bowl. Remove the cartilage (lump crabmeat doesn't have much). Add the celery, onion, green pepper, mayonnaise, Old Bay, and bread crumbs and stir together gently with your hands so as not to break up the crab too much. Add more mayonnaise if the mixture looks too dry.

Shape the mixture into 8 patties about the size of the palm of your hand. If you are cooking the crab cakes immediately, dredge them in the cornmeal. If not, you can store the crabmeat mixture in a covered container in the refrigerator until ready to cook (up to 2 hours) and dredge them just before cooking.

Heat the oil in a large skillet over medium-high heat until it shimmers. Don't use too much oil; it should reach only halfway up the side of the crab cakes. Gently place the crab cakes in the pan and fry on one side until browned, about 2–3 minutes. Carefully flip over the crab cakes and fry them on the other side until they are golden brown. Drain the cakes on a paper towel and transfer them to a warm platter. Serve with your preferred sauce.

NOTE ❄ Buy the crabmeat the day of or the day before cooking because fresh crabmeat perishes quickly. Jumbo lump or lump crabmeat makes for the best crab cakes. The meat is pricey, but it's worth it for this special meal.

Herb Roasted Pork Tenderloin with Fig Chutney

My family loves pork. This tenderloin dish is flavorful, and the meat is succulent. I usually cook two tenderloins at a time: one for Sunday dinner and the other for Monday leftovers, which make for great pork sandwiches on slider rolls.

MAKES 6 SERVINGS FOR SUNDAY DINNER,
PLUS LEFTOVERS

FOR THE MEAT

2 pork tenderloins
Salt and black pepper, to taste
8 tablespoons Herbes de Provence
Olive oil for browning

FOR THE CHUTNEY

1 teaspoon olive oil
⅓ cup diced red bell pepper
⅓ cup diced onions
⅓ cup diced celery
1 cup cranberries
1 teaspoon allspice
¼ cup balsamic vinegar
1 tablespoon minced garlic
¼ cup brown sugar
8 medium Black Mission figs, diced
1 medium Golden Delicious apple, peeled and diced
Crushed red pepper, to taste
3 tablespoons port wine

To prepare the tenderloins, season liberally with salt and pepper and the Herbes de Provence pressing to get the herbs to adhere to the pork. Place the tenderloins in a plastic bag, seal the bag, squeezing out the air, and let marinate overnight in the refrigerator.

Set the meat on the counter for at least 30 minutes to bring it to room temperature before you are ready to cook it.

Preheat the oven to 400°.

Heat the olive oil in a large ovenproof skillet on medium-high. Place the pork in the skillet and sear the meat on all sides. Transfer the pan to the oven. For medium-rare, cook for about 15 minutes. For medium, cook for 20 minutes.

Remove the pork from the oven and let it rest.

To make the chutney, heat the olive oil in a saucepan; add the peppers, onions, and celery and sauté until tender. Add the cranberries and cook until tender. Add the allspice, vinegar, garlic, and sugar. Heat through until the sugar has dissolved. Toss in the figs and apples and season with crushed red pepper. Add the port wine and let simmer about 5 minutes or until heated through.

Thinly slice the pork and place it on a platter; spoon the chutney over the slices. Serve warm.

Eye of Round Pot Roast with Baby Portabellas

There is nothing more inviting to any large group than comfort food. My sister Bernie's roast recipe evokes days gone by when the smell of a hearty meal met you at the front door, especially on a winter's afternoon, and enticed you in to sit awhile and visit with family and friends. This dish, cooked for hours in a rich gravy, delivers for both Sunday dinners and large family gatherings with its sheer deliciousness.

MAKES 10 SERVINGS

1 (5-pound) eye of round roast

1 teaspoon salt

1 tablespoon coarsely ground black pepper

All-purpose flour for dusting

Olive oil for browning

1 large yellow or white onion, quartered

3 celery stalks with leaves on, washed well, sliced into chunks

4 whole carrots, halved lengthwise and cut into 2-inch pieces

½ pound baby portabella mushrooms, stems removed, sliced

1 tablespoon minced garlic

2 cups water

1 cup red wine

¼ cup all-purpose flour or cornstarch

1 tablespoon Kitchen Bouquet (a browning and seasoning sauce)

Preheat the oven to 350°.

Wash the roast and pat it dry. Mix the salt and pepper together and then season the meat with it. Dust the meat with the flour. Heat the olive oil in a large skillet over medium-high heat. Place the roast in the pan and brown on all sides.

Place the roast in the center of a large oval roaster pan and arrange the onions, celery, carrots, and mushrooms around it. Rub the garlic all over the roast.

Pour the water and red wine into the roaster, cover the pan, and cook for 90 minutes. Remove the roast from the pan and place it on a cutting board or plate to rest.

Reduce the oven temperature to 325°. While the meat is cooling, strain the liquid from the pan through a colander into a saucepan and reserve the vegetables. Add the flour or cornstarch and the Kitchen Bouquet and stir until smooth; bring the liquid to a light simmer to thicken. You can add more flour or cornstarch for a thicker gravy and adjust Kitchen Bouquet to preferred richness of gravy color.

Slice the roast into serving portions and return the meat to the roaster with any leftover juices. Return the reserved vegetables to the pan and pour the gravy over all.

Cook the roast for another 30–45 minutes or until fork-tender. Serve with mashed potatoes.

NOTE ❋ My family prefers this meat sliced on the thin side.

Roasted Turkey Breast with Winter Vegetables

A turkey breast is perfect for Sunday dinner, especially during the cold months. This entrée is easy to make and great for dinner, leftovers, and sandwiches. The turkey drippings and the seasonings will pack a flavor punch to the winter vegetables. You can serve this dish with or without gravy. You can also reserve some turkey for a pot pie for later.

MAKES 8 SERVINGS

- 1 pound butternut squash, cut into 1-inch pieces
- 1 pound carrots, peeled and cut into 1-inch pieces
- 1 pound parsnips, peeled and cut into 1-inch pieces
- 1 red onion, peeled and quartered
- 1 tablespoon plus 2 teaspoons extra-virgin olive oil, divided
- 1 teaspoon balsamic vinegar
- 1 teaspoon salt, divided
- 1 teaspoon dried Italian seasoning, divided
- $\frac{1}{2}$ teaspoon black pepper, divided
- 1 boneless turkey breast with skin (about $3\frac{1}{2}$ pounds)

Preheat the oven to 325°.

Place the squash, carrots, parsnips, and onions in a large roasting pan and toss with 1 tablespoon of the olive oil and the balsamic vinegar. Season with ½ teaspoon of the salt, ½ teaspoon of the Italian seasoning, and ¼ teaspoon of the pepper.

Rub the turkey with the remaining 2 teaspoons of olive oil and season with the remaining salt, the Italian seasoning, and the pepper. Press the turkey into the vegetables. Roast for 70 minutes or until the juices run clear and an instant-read meat thermometer inserted into the thickest part of the breast reads 165°.

Remove the pan from the oven and cover loosely with foil. Let the turkey rest for 15 minutes (see Note). If you choose to make gravy, this would be the time.

Slice the turkey and serve with the roasted vegetables.

NOTE ❊ If the vegetables aren't fork-tender at this point, remove the turkey to a platter and cover loosely with foil. While it rests, roast the vegetables for an additional 10–15 minutes.

Fragrant Sunday Chicken with Olives and Apricots

You won't have to call anyone to Sunday dinner after they smell the sweet scent of prunes, apricots, and olives in this fragrant chicken dish. This entrée is great for a snowy Sunday afternoon because it yields plenty of leftovers for another meal.

MAKES 6 SERVINGS FOR SUNDAY DINNER,
PLUS LEFTOVERS

---

1 head garlic, peeled and finely pureed

¾ cup chopped fresh oregano

1 teaspoon coarse salt

1 teaspoon black pepper

½ cup red wine vinegar

½ cup olive oil

½ cup pitted prunes

½ cup dried apricots

½ cup green, Kalamata, and prune olives

4 ounces capers with some of the juice

6 bone-in chicken breasts, cut in half

30 chicken wing drumettes

1 cup finely packed light-brown sugar

1 cup white wine

In a large bowl, combine the garlic, oregano, salt, pepper, vinegar, olive oil, prunes, apricots, olives, and capers. Pour the marinade into a large plastic lidded container. Add the chicken pieces and marinate overnight.

Preheat the oven to 350°. In a 9 × 13-inch casserole arrange the chicken in a single layer and pour in the marinade. Sprinkle the chicken with the brown sugar and pour the wine around the sides of the casserole. Bake for 50 minutes, basting periodically with pan juices.

Serve hot or warm with rice.

NOTE ❋ I like to serve the breasts for dinner and save the wing drumettes for another meal.

Papa's Picnic Ham with Jack Daniels and Cloves

My aunt Shirley of Lynchburg, Virginia, still recalls the time when she first started dating her husband, my uncle Moco, when she arrived at his house just as her future father-in-law, Papa, was finishing one of his picnic hams. "He was trimming off the fat. It was one of the prettiest things I ever saw Mr. Moore cook." His ham was a beauty, scored and decorated with cloves. I remember once he made me a picnic ham and packed it for my return to Howard University, where I lived in a dormitory with a kitchen. He even gave me a knife and showed me how to slice it. Thin. This recipe is a combination of his ham along with some modern-day touches from my mother. When I was growing up, family members often cooked their ham on the stovetop in a pan. But my mother now produces this family classic by cooking the ham in the oven.

MAKES 16–20 SERVINGS

1 (8- to 10-pound) picnic ham
Whole cloves for decorating
½ cup Jack Daniels bourbon
1 cup brown sugar

Preheat the oven to 325°.

Place about an inch of water in the bottom of a big roasting pan fitted with a rack. Place the whole pork shoulder package in the sink to remove it from the packaging, including the netting.

Place the ham, skin-side up, on the rack in the pan and bake until the skin is golden and crackling and the internal temperature at the bone is 160°, about 2½–3 hours. Remove the ham from the oven, cover lightly with foil, and let rest at least 20 minutes or cool enough to handle.

With a sharp knife, remove the layer of skin and fat from the meat. Make shallow cuts (about ½ inch deep) in the ham from top to bottom spaced 1 inch apart. Score the ham diagonally across the first set of cuts. Place the cloves where the scores cross.

Combine the Jack Daniels and brown sugar in a small bowl to make a paste. Apply the mixture with a pastry brush to the ham. Return the meat to the hot oven, uncovered, and bake for about 15–30 minutes or until a meat thermometer placed in the thickest part of the meat reaches a temperature of 170°.

Short Ribs

One of my father's favorite winter dinners was beef short ribs. My mother prepared them by cooking them in the oven. I like to use the slow cooker instead for these meaty beef ribs. I often chop the vegetables the night before and store them in a plastic bag for early morning Sunday cooking.

MAKES 6 SERVINGS

½ cup olive oil
4 pounds beef short ribs
Salt and black pepper, to taste
1 cup all-purpose flour
2 cups chopped onions
1 cup chopped celery
1 cup chopped carrots
2 tablespoons minced garlic
1 tablespoon dried thyme
1 cup red wine
1 cup beef stock

Heat the oil in a large pot over medium-high heat. Season the ribs with salt and pepper and dredge them in flour. Sear the ribs in the oil in small batches and set aside.

In the same pot, add the onions and sauté for 2 minutes. Add the celery and carrots and cook for 2 minutes. Season the vegetables with salt and pepper and add the garlic and thyme.

Transfer the short ribs and sautéed vegetables to an oval slow cooker. Deglaze the large pot with the red wine, scraping up all the bits on the bottom. Add that to the slow cooker along with the beef stock. Cook the short ribs for 6–8 hours on low. Remove the short ribs from the slow cooker. With an immersion blender, purée the vegetables into the rich red wine sauce, creating an even chunkier sauce. If you need more liquid for the sauce, add additional beef broth and or red wine. Serve over Classic Buttery Mashed Potatoes (page 57).

NOTE ✳ Ask the butcher for well-marbled, meaty ribs firmly attached to the bone without a huge amount of surface fat.

Pork Chops with Onion Gravy

There's nothing like a fried pork chop simmered in gravy with onions. I like to taste a little onion in every bite. My mother and grandmother always fried what seemed like a mountain of pork chops. Sometimes pork chops can be tough, but this method surely makes them fork-tender. There were never leftovers of this family favorite.

MAKES 6 SERVINGS

6 center-cut pork chops, 1 inch thick

Grill Mates Montreal Steak Seasoning (a coarse salt,
    black pepper, and spice blend), to taste

1½ cups plus 2 tablespoons all-purpose flour, divided

2 cups vegetable oil

1–2 cups hot water

1 cup chicken broth

1 large Vidalia onion, peeled and sliced thin

Kitchen Bouquet

Salt and black pepper, to taste

Wash the pork chops and season with the steak seasoning. Season 1½ cups of the flour as well and dredge the pork chops in the flour mixture.

Heat the oil in a large skillet over medium-high heat. In batches, fry the pork chops for 4–5 minutes per side. Drain the chops on a paper towel.

Discard most of the oil from the frying pan, leaving the dredges in the bottom. Slowly add the hot water to the pan; add the chicken broth and whisk in the remaining flour. Add the onions and a little bit of Kitchen Bouquet for color. Season with salt and pepper. The gravy will be thin at this point.

Return the chops to the pan and simmer on a low heat for 20 minutes. The gravy will thicken up. Serve hot.

NOTE ❋ My family loves onions, so we often add more than one onion. You can also add mushrooms. My mother prefers her pork chops thicker and often uses boneless loin chops, especially if they are on sale.

Sundried Tomato, Artichoke, and Spinach Quiche

Quiche is most familiar as an elegant brunch dish, and its custardy base can showcase strong flavors. This savory quiche is easy to make and perfect to serve with a salad for Sunday supper. This vegetarian pie makes perfect leftovers.

MAKES 1 (9-INCH) QUICHE

1 9-inch piecrust, unbaked

2 cups sautéed spinach

1 cup drained and chopped artichoke hearts

½ cup chopped sundried tomatoes

⅓ cup pitted olives

3 large eggs

1 cup half-and-half

2 cups grated cheese, such as Swiss, cheddar, or Gruyère, or crumbled feta

½ teaspoon salt

½ teaspoon black pepper

Preheat the oven to 350°. Place the spinach, artichoke hearts, sundried tomatoes, and olives in the piecrust, making sure that the sundried tomatoes and olives are evenly distributed.

In a medium bowl, whisk together the eggs and half-and-half. Stir in 1 cup of the cheese and the salt and pepper. Pour the mixture into the piecrust. Add the remaining cheese. Bake for 45 minutes or until the filling is set.

NOTE ❊ Choose fresh and flavorful ingredients that are in season. Be creative—only your imagination limits what can go in a quiche. If you have lots of squash or zucchini, use them. I do like making them colorful. If you want to make the quiche less caloric, strongly flavored cheeses like feta or chèvre are good choices because the more intense the flavor, the less cheese you need.

Sides

When I was growing up, side dishes meant comfort food and the best seasonal fare—often from Papa's garden or a farmer's market. These palette pleasers include my mother's potato salad, corn pudding, and green beans with fingerling potatoes, all southern classics.

Slow Cooker Mac and Cheese

Macaroni and cheese is one of the quintessential southern sides. This is easy to make and is a great dish to bring to someone's table for Sunday supper, especially since it's easily transported in a slow cooker. This recipe produces the rich and creamy taste of traditional mac and cheese without taking up valuable space in your oven on the week's busiest cooking day. I especially like it during the cold months. This slow cooker recipe comes from a former newsroom coworker, copy editor Pam Nelson. Members of the features department of the newspaper were always having potlucks, and this was one of our favorite dishes.

MAKES 8–10 SERVINGS

---

8 ounces elbow macaroni

4 cups shredded sharp cheddar cheese

1 (12-ounce) can evaporated milk

1½ cups milk

2 eggs

1 teaspoon salt

½ teaspoon black pepper

Nonstick cooking spray

In a large pot, boil the macaroni until it is cooked al dente. Drain the pasta and place it in a large bowl. Add 3 cups of the cheese and the evaporated milk, milk, eggs, and salt and pepper.

Spray the slow cooker with nonstick cooking spray. Transfer the macaroni and cheese mixture to the slow cooker. Sprinkle the mixture with the remaining cheese.

Cook the mac and cheese on low for 4 hours or until the mixture is firm and golden around the edges (see Note). Do not remove the cover or stir the mixture until it has finished cooking.

NOTE ❋ Some slow cookers cook faster than others. You'll want to check this recipe around the 3½-hour mark.

Esther's Summer Potato Salad

My mother started making potato salad when she was a girl. The oldest of four children, she made it Sunday after church and would make enough to fill the large vegetable compartment at the bottom of the refrigerator. Her father, my beloved Papa, a blue-collar worker, often carried the potato salad in a mayonnaise jar for his lunch. My mother was a Moore, and many Moore family gatherings were marked by this classic summer salad. "My love of potato salad came from watching my aunt Shirley make it and smelling it in my grandmother's kitchen," she says. The scent of fresh-cut celery, onions, and pickles drew her closer to the bowl. "We always ate it when it wasn't ice cold. That's why I like it today when it's just made."

MAKES 6–8 SERVINGS

6 medium white potatoes
1 cup chopped celery
1 white onion, chopped
½ cup pimentos
5–6 sweet pickles, chopped
3 hard-boiled eggs, grated
5 tablespoons Hellman's mayonnaise
2 teaspoons prepared yellow mustard
2 teaspoons cider vinegar
1 teaspoon sugar
Salt and black pepper, to taste
Paprika for garnish

Wash and peel the potatoes and cut them in small, uniform chunks. Put the potatoes in a pot and cover them with water. Boil until fork-tender, about 20–25 minutes. Drain the potatoes in a colander and let cool, about 30 minutes or so. You want them warm but not hot.

Transfer the potatoes to a large bowl and add the celery, onions, pimentos, and pickles.

In a separate bowl, combine the grated eggs, mayonnaise, mustard, vinegar, and sugar. Taste it. Adjust the seasonings to your taste.

Gently combine this mixture with the potato salad. Season with salt and pepper. Sprinkle with paprika and serve.

Scalloped Potatoes

My father, James Anderson Lacy, loved scalloped potatoes. My mother only prepared this dish on Sundays even though my sisters and I loved it so much that we'd almost race home from school to eat the leftovers. This dish combines three of my family's favorite ingredients, potatoes, extra-sharp cheddar cheese, and onions. It's simple to make and easy to assemble. The key to this dish is making sure the potatoes are thoroughly cooked, meaning fork-tender. I still love to eat the leftovers the next day.

MAKES 6 SERVINGS

4–6 Yukon Gold potatoes

2 small yellow onions

12 ounces extra-sharp cheddar cheese

1 teaspoon salt, divided

1 teaspoon black pepper, divided

3 tablespoons salted butter, cut into small pieces

1½ cups milk (more or less depending on the size of your pan)

Preheat the oven to 350°. Wash and peel the potatoes and peel the onions. Thinly slice both using a mandolin. With a sharp knife, thinly slice the cheese. Place half of the potatoes in a single layer in a 2-quart casserole dish and sprinkle with ½ teaspoon each of the salt and pepper. Place half of the onions in a single layer over the potatoes, and arrange half of cheese over the onions. Dot the cheese with half the butter, and repeat the layering with the remaining potatoes, onions, cheese, and butter.

Add the milk and sprinkle the top layer with the remaining salt and pepper.

Bake uncovered for about 1 hour. Be careful not to pour too much milk in this dish because it will boil over and spill in the oven. The milk should cover only ½ of the layers in the pan. Serve hot.

NOTE ❋ I line the oven rack beneath the casserole with aluminum foil in case the liquid spills.

Sweet Potato Casserole
with Pecan Topping

In the black church, a meal often comes with the sermon. I tasted this fabulous mashed sweet potato dish topped with pecans during the church's holiday progressive dinner. That's where every course was served at a different host's home. I loved this side dish so much that I asked the cook to share her recipe. This dish is a true blessing.

MAKES 6–8 SERVINGS

FOR THE CASSEROLE

4–5 sweet potatoes

3 eggs

$\frac{1}{2}$ cup evaporated milk

$\frac{3}{4}$ cup salted butter, at room temperature

$2\frac{1}{2}$ cups sugar

1 teaspoon ground cinnamon

1 teaspoon nutmeg

2 teaspoons vanilla extract

FOR THE TOPPING

$\frac{1}{2}$ cup brown sugar

$\frac{1}{2}$ cup all-purpose flour

$\frac{1}{2}$ cup salted butter, at room temperature

1 cup chopped pecans

Preheat the oven to 350°.

To prepare the casserole, boil the sweet potatoes until tender. Drain the water and peel the potatoes. Using an electric mixer, beat the sweet potatoes, eggs, evaporated milk, butter, sugar, cinnamon, nutmeg, and vanilla until smooth. Transfer to a 9 × 13-inch casserole dish.

To prepare the topping, mix the brown sugar and flour in a medium bowl. Cut in the butter until the mixture is coarse. Stir in the pecans.

Sprinkle the mixture over the sweet potato casserole. Bake for 30 minutes or until the topping is lightly browned.

Savory Stuffed Crookneck Squash

In the South, squash is abundant in the summer. I'm often sup-plied with this seasonal vegetable by coworkers, neighbors, friends, and the farmers' market.

As a child, I didn't like squash much. It was often tasteless, wa-tery, and mushy, and prepared with very little seasoning.

This squash is wonderfully flavorful. I like going to the farm-ers' market with my mother early on a Saturday morning and letting her pick out a few gourds. "I like the little ones," she says. "They don't have those big seeds." She also advises picking uni-formly small ones so that all of the squash will be ready at the same time. This dish goes nicely with Pork Chops with Onion Gravy (page 32).

MAKES 4–6 SERVINGS

---

6 small crookneck squash
¹⁄₂ teaspoon olive oil
6 slices bacon
¹⁄₂ cup finely chopped onions
¹⁄₂ cup bread crumbs
¹⁄₂ cup shredded sharp white cheddar cheese
Olive oil, for drizzling
Salt and black pepper, to taste

Preheat the oven for 10 minutes at 450°. Wash the squash, cut in half lengthwise, and brush with olive oil. Place the squash face down on a cookie sheet and bake for 5 minutes. Remove the pan from the oven and let the squash cool slightly. Gently scoop out the pulp with a spoon. Reserve the pulp. Set the squash shells aside.

Turn down the oven temperature to 400°.

Fry the bacon slices in a large skillet until crisp. Drain the pan, leaving a light coating of grease. Set the bacon aside. Add the onions to the pan. Cook about 2 minutes on medium-low heat until the onions are translucent. Add the pulp to the pan and mash it in with the onions. Add the bread crumbs and cheese and let the cheese melt.

Divide the mixture among the squash halves. Chop the bacon and sprinkle it over the stuffing. Sprinkle the squash with a few additional bread crumbs and lightly drizzle with olive oil. Bake for 15–20 minutes or until the tops are browned.

Golden Hot Pepper Jelly

I was pleasantly surprised one day when I found a box filled with homemade goodies on my front porch from my handyman Mike Richardson of Raleigh, North Carolina. Along with pickles and blueberry jelly was his delicious, spicy-hot, golden pepper jelly, a mix of delicately mild apricots and veggies. Tiny pieces of onion and peppers infuse in this sweet and sour jelly.

Mike received a white ribbon at the North Carolina State Fair for this tasty condiment. What a perfect little house gift that can be enjoyed anytime. This reminded me of how Papa would often give Sunday dinner guests some home-canned goods to take home. I love southern hospitality. It really feeds the soul.

Enjoy this with different kinds of cheeses or on pieces of succulent meats.

MAKES 6 HALF-PINT JARS

1 (18-ounce) jar apricot jam
¼ cup finely diced red onions
¼ cup finely diced green bell peppers
¼ cup finely diced red bell peppers
2 cups sugar
1½ cups apple cider vinegar
4–6 habanero peppers, seeded and finely diced
2 jalapeños, seeded and finely diced
1 tablespoon red pepper flakes
½ tablespoon butter (to minimize foaming)
1 box no-sugar-added pectin

Prepare 6 half-pint jars and lids for canning (see Note). Combine all the ingredients, except for the pectin, in a stainless steel pot. Bring the mixture to a good boil, stirring frequently, to prevent sticking. Stir in the pectin and bring the jelly back to a rolling boil. After 90 seconds, remove the jelly from heat and pour it into the prepared jars.

NOTE ❋ To learn about safe canning practices, you can find information at the National Center for Home Food Preservation website.

Roasted Vegetable Medley

Any day of the week my friends Mary Miller and Bob Geolas of Raleigh, North Carolina, may be having Sunday dinner. They have an open kitchen policy; everyone, whether it is one of their four children or a friend, is welcome to stir the pot in their home. On one of those evenings, Mary's brother, Stephen Miller of Raleigh, brought a wonderful medley of asparagus and Brussels sprouts marinated in olive oil. The roasting process brings out their natural sweetness and brilliant color. Stephen sometimes adds sweet potatoes, Yukon Gold potatoes, and red potatoes to the dish so everyone will have something they like, he says. "The roasting gives the vegetables a smoky, deep flavor and makes for a great display; . . . it takes all the bitterness out of the Brussels sprouts. When you roast them, they are delicious."

MAKES 6–8 SERVINGS

1 pound Brussels sprouts
1 pound asparagus
Olive oil
2 sweet potatoes
3 Yukon Gold potatoes
6 red potatoes
Salt and black pepper or your favorite seasoning, such as
    Herbes de Provence, to taste

Trim off the bad leaves of the Brussels sprouts. Break the ends off of the asparagus. Rinse the vegetables and place them in a plastic bag. Pour enough olive oil over the vegetables to coat.

Rinse and peel the sweet and Yukon Gold potatoes and cut them into chunks that are slightly smaller than the Brussels sprouts. Cut the unpeeled red potatoes into small chunks. (All of the potatoes should be the same size so they will cook evenly.) Place the potatoes in another plastic bag and pour enough olive oil over them to coat.

Marinate the vegetables and potatoes for 1 hour in the refrigerator, turning the bags occasionally to make sure all of the vegetables are getting a liberal coating.

Remove the bags from the refrigerator and bring the vegetables to room temperature. Preheat the oven to 400°.

Line a large baking pan with aluminum foil (the pan should be large enough to accommodate the vegetables in a single layer). Add the potatoes and Brussels sprouts (leaving enough space to add the asparagus in a single layer). Season the vegetables with salt and pepper or your favorite seasoning. Roast for 10–15 minutes.

Remove the pan from the oven and add the asparagus; season with salt and pepper. Add more olive oil to the pan if the vegetables look too dry and return the pan to the oven. Bake for an additional 10 minutes.

Steven likes the sprouts and asparagus a little al dente because they will continue to cook for a few minutes after you remove them from the oven.

Transfer to a dish and serve hot.

NOTE ❊ If you want to add more intense flavor, Stephen suggests drizzling balsamic vinegar over the vegetables or adding some Parmesan cheese shavings just before serving. Of course, you can add both.

Butternut Squash with Sage

This is a delightful and easy side dish that combines the rich sweetness of butternut squash with the sharp, savory scent and rough texture of sage. The roasting process caramelizes the squash and makes it sweet. The honey is for those who like extra sweetness. That would be me. This recipe comes from my writing buddy, author Marjorie Hudson of Pittsboro, North Carolina, who grows her own butternut squash. I meet quarterly with a group of writers for Sunday brunch, which is Sunday dinner for us that day.

MAKES 6 SERVINGS

---

2 large butternut squash

3 tablespoons olive oil

1 tablespoon honey (optional)

3 fresh sage sprigs (about 2 inches long)

1–2 teaspoons kosher salt

Preheat the oven to 400°.

Wash, peel, and cut the squash in half lengthwise; scoop out the seeds with a spoon and cut the squash into 1-inch chunks. Toss the squash pieces in a bowl with the oil and honey.

Spread the squash in a single layer on 2 greased baking sheets. Bake for 50 minutes, stirring occasionally, until the squash is nicely caramelized and fork-tender.

While the squash roasts, wash the sage and pat it dry with paper towels. Pull the leaves from the stems of 2 of the sprigs and reserve the remaining sprig for garnish. Place 1 leaf on top of the other, roll them lengthwise into a cigar shape, thinly slice them, then mince the slices.

Place the squash in a shallow serving dish and sprinkle lightly with kosher salt and the chopped sage, then garnish with the remaining sage sprig.

NOTE ✷ About growing sage and butternut squash Marjorie says, "Sage likes good drainage and a light soil. It will grow over the winter with some protection in the South. Butternut squash is easy to grow. It needs room to spread and is a prolific producer. I like the Waltham variety, it's a good keeper, with a beautiful tawny skin, straight neck, and deep orange flesh."

Collard Greens

Collards taste better after the first fall frost. I like to get up early on a Saturday morning and go to the farmers' market and pick out a nice batch with sturdy, dark green leaves. I prefer baby collards, the leaves are smaller and more tender. Avoid worm-eaten leaves. My family believes collards are the foundation for meals to come during the week. My mother loves to cook a large pot of these green leafy vegetables and freeze some of them in plastic bags for later use.

MAKES 8 SERVINGS

1 quart low-sodium chicken broth

2 smoked turkey wings or drumsticks

2 teaspoons spice blend (salt, black pepper, crushed red pepper, and garlic powder)

3 pounds collard greens, washed and chopped

1 teaspoon sugar (optional)

Salt and black pepper, to taste

In a large pot, bring 1 quart of chicken broth to a boil and add the smoked meat and spice blend. Reduce the heat to medium and cook for 30 minutes.

Wash the collard greens and remove most of the stems (I like leaving in a few for texture). Stack 2–3 leaves on top of one another, roll up, and cut into ½-inch-wide pieces.

Transfer the greens to the pot. Simmer, covered, for 45–60 minutes on medium-low heat or until tender to your liking. Periodically use tongs to lift the greens on the bottom of the pot to the top. If the collards are bitter, add the sugar. Season with salt and pepper.

NOTE ❋ These are even better served with apple cider vinegar and chopped onions.

Green Beans with Fingerling Potatoes

This Sunday supper staple is one of my favorites. I have fond memories of sitting at the red Formica table with my grandmother as we snapped the ends off the beans. Lots of conversation and laughter was exchanged between Grandma and me. My family normally cooked the green beans with white potatoes. Recently, during a visit to my mother's house in Washington, D.C., she made this southern side with fingerling potatoes. My family loves this starch. My mother always says, "We are Virginians. We are potato people." So she loads the dish with potatoes so the leftovers are not just the green beans. And don't skimp on the butter, which really intensifies that good flavor of the green beans and potatoes.

MAKES 6 SERVINGS

1½ pounds fresh green beans

10–11 fingerling potatoes

3 cups chicken broth

½ tablespoon Herbes de Provence

Salt and black pepper, to taste

2–3 pats salted butter

Rinse the green beans, snap off the ends, and break the beans into bite-sized pieces. Place the green beans and potatoes in a large pot and add the chicken broth. Cover the pot and cook the vegetables on medium-high heat for 30 minutes, periodically stirring them with a slotted spoon. Add the Herbes de Provence and season with salt and pepper. Cook for 10 more minutes or until the beans and potatoes are tender. Transfer to a serving dish and add the butter.

NOTE ✻ Green beans and collards are sides you can build other meals around during the work week. This recipe pairs well with fried chicken on Sunday and fried fish on Monday. My mother also loves this dish for a quick lunch with the Cucumber Tomato Salad (page 65).

Sweet and Spicy Corn Cakes

My friend Dana Wynne Lindquist of Raleigh, North Carolina, spends her summers in northern Michigan. The summer of 2012, she decided to master creating these sweet and mildly spicy corn cakes. When fresh corn was in season, she made these weekly and enjoyed combining the leftovers with various meals throughout the week. Her summer neighbors loved them and have come up with their own serving ideas: a dollop of guacamole and sour cream or honey mustard on top to create an appetizer. She learned from an Argentinian friend that her mother served similar corn cakes with ham and melted cheese on top for a lunch treat. Yum.

MAKES 18–24 CORN CAKES

---

2 cups finely ground cornmeal

1 cup bleached all-purpose flour (gluten-free flour substitute
also works as well)

1½ teaspoons baking powder

1 teaspoon black pepper

1 tablespoon salt

2 cups fresh corn

1–2 tablespoons honey

1 (15-ounce) can black beans, drained

1 large Vidalia onion, minced

1 large green bell pepper, minced

1 large red bell pepper, minced

1 tablespoon diced pickled jalapeños (more may be added
for more heat)

3 eggs, at room temperature

Good-quality olive oil for frying

Melted butter (optional)

Sift together the dry ingredients into a large bowl. Set aside.

In a separate bowl, combine the corn and honey. Add the black beans, onions, bell peppers, and jalapeños. Add the dry ingredients to the vegetable mix.

In a small bowl, beat the eggs. Fold them into the mixture until all the vegetables are evenly covered.

Heat a large skillet over medium-high heat. Coat the pan with a thin layer of olive oil. Form the corn mixture into 2- to 3-inch patties, about ½ inch thick (see Note). Cook on each side for 2–3 minutes or until lightly browned. If desired, butter may be drizzled on each cake before final turning.

NOTE ✽ If the mixture is too wet to form into cakes, add a little flour—just enough to hold the cakes together. Sometimes Dana adds 2–3 cloves of garlic or more jalapeños depending on how spicy she wants them. If you want crispier corn cakes, add more olive oil to the skillet and cook at a higher heat. These freeze well and can be quickly thawed if unexpected guests stop by for a visit.

Corn Pudding

My mother often craves her mother-in-law's sweet and savory corn pudding. The two women shared the same first name, Esther, as well as their love for this soothing southern classic. Corn pudding makes for a great starchy side, perfect with a piece of Grandma's Fried Chicken (page 17).

MAKES 6–8 SERVINGS

3 tablespoons unsalted butter

3 tablespoons all-purpose flour

¾ cup sugar

2 eggs

1 cup milk

1 (16-ounce) can whole kernel corn, drained

1 (15-ounce) can cream-style corn

1 teaspoon vanilla extract

½ teaspoon salt

Preheat the oven to 350°. Place the butter in a 1½- or 2-quart casserole and place in the oven to melt. Tilt the casserole, making sure the butter coats the pan evenly. Set aside.

Combine the flour and sugar in a bowl. Add the eggs and whip until fluffy. Add the milk, corn, vanilla, and salt and stir until well combined. Pour the mixture into the prepared casserole.

Bake for 1 hour, stirring after 30 minutes to make sure that the corn doesn't sink to the bottom of the dish. Test for doneness by inserting a knife in the center. The knife should come out clean.

Classic Buttery Mashed Potatoes

When I was growing up, we used white potatoes for mashed potatoes, but the Canadian bred Yukon Gold potato has become one of my favorites. These yellow-fleshed beauties create a buttery mashed potato without a lot of work.

MAKES 6 SERVINGS

6–8 medium Yukon Gold potatoes
2–2$\frac{1}{2}$ cups chicken broth
1 cup milk
4 tablespoons salted butter
Coarse salt and black pepper, to taste
Chopped fresh chives, for garnish

Wash, peel, and cut the potatoes in quarters. Place them in a pot, add the chicken broth, and boil for 20–30 minutes or until tender. Drain the chicken broth from the pot.

Heat the milk in a microwave for 30 seconds or until hot. Slowly add the hot milk to the potatoes. Mix with a hand blender until the potatoes are creamy. Cut the butter into small pieces and add to the potatoes. Season with salt and pepper, garnish with the chives, and serve hot.

NOTE ❋ Papa stored his potatoes under the house in a cellar complete with shelves with dividers separating his onions from root vegetables. I try to buy potatoes only a day before I'm ready to cook them. I find my kitchen is too warm to store them in a vegetable bin. They tend to start sprouting. If they are stored in the refrigerator, the potatoes often become sweeter, altering the good natural flavor. For good mashed potatoes, you want to start with the best raw ingredient from the start.

Salads

Salads prepared with seasonal fruits and vegetables make quick and easy additions to the big dinner. These salads can be prepared ahead of time so there's one less thing to do on Sunday.

Sweet and Crunchy Broccoli Salad

This sweet and crunchy salad is easy to make and packs a lot of flavor. It's nice to have a combination of quick dishes to make as well as more complicated ones for Sunday dinner. The key to this salad is buying the freshest broccoli available. My mother often asks the produce man to go in the back and get her a couple of fresh bunches.

MAKES 8–10 SERVINGS

---

2 bunches fresh broccoli, heads and stalks
1 large red onion, chopped
1½ cups shredded sharp cheddar cheese
½ cup mayonnaise
3 tablespoons sugar
2 tablespoons apple cider vinegar

Wash the broccoli and remove the small leaves. Cut the heads into bite-size pieces. Skin the stalks with a vegetable peeler. Place the florets and a few stalks in a large bowl. Chop a few of the medium stalks and add them to give the salad more color and texture. Add the onions and cheese.

In a small bowl, combine the mayonnaise, sugar, and vinegar. Whisk together until smooth. Taste and adjust the seasonings; if too sweet, add more mayonnaise and vinegar.

Gradually pour the dressing over the broccoli mixture and toss gently to coat, being careful not to oversaturate the salad (see Note).

Chill and serve.

NOTE ✳ I follow my mother's lead when adding dressing to most salads. It's best to add it gradually to avoid adding too much and making your salad soggy.

Summer Fruit Salad

This summery salad is naturally sweet, cool, colorful, and refreshing. The key is to buy the fruit a couple of days before you plan to serve it so that all the ingredients will be at their peak ripeness. This salad pairs well with a green salad and Mama's Meaty Crab Cakes (page 18).

MAKES 6–8 SERVINGS

1 seedless watermelon, about 3–4 pounds
2 cups sliced strawberries
4 ripe mangoes
2 tablespoons fig balsamic vinegar
Spearmint leaves, for garnish

Wash the watermelon. Place it on a cutting board and cut off both ends. Turn the watermelon so it sits flat on one of the cut ends. Slice off the watermelon's rind and then flip the fruit over and carefully slice off any remaining rind and white parts. Cut the watermelon in half from top to bottom. Place each half cut-side down and slice them in rows lengthwise, then cut across, creating chunks of watermelon. Toss the melon pieces in a bowl.

Rinse the strawberries. Pick off the green tops. Place each berry onto its side. Cut the berry in thin slices from the top, working your way down to the bottom and creating round, thin slices. Add the slices to the bowl.

Wash the mangoes. To cut, hold a mango on the cutting board, stem end down. Place your knife about ¼ inch from the widest part of the mango (to avoid cutting into the pit) and cut straight down. Rotate the mango and repeat this cut on the other side. Cut parallel slices into the mango flesh, being careful not to cut through the skin. Turn the mango cheek to make perpendicular slices to make a checkerboard pattern. Turn the scored mango cheek inside out by pushing the skin up from underneath and scrape the mango chunks off of the skin with a knife into the bowl.

Drizzle the fig balsamic vinegar over the fruit mixture, tossing to coat.

Chill for at least 30 minutes. Add spearmint leaves for garnish and serve.

Roasted Pears, Walnuts, and Dried Cherries

This is a gorgeous fall salad with pears, walnuts, and dried cherries. This decadent seasonal salad almost tastes like dessert.

MAKES 6 SERVINGS

3 ripe, firm red Anjou pears

$1/4$ cup fresh lemon juice, plus more for sprinkling on the pears

3 ounces crumbled sharp blue cheese

$1/4$ cup dried cherries

$1/4$ cup walnuts, toasted and chopped

$1/2$ cup apple juice

3 tablespoons Madeira wine

3 tablespoons light brown sugar, packed

$1/4$ cup extra-virgin olive oil

$7^1/2$ ounces spring salad mix

Salt and black pepper, to taste

Preheat the oven to 375°.

Peel the pears and cut in half lengthwise. Use a melon baller to remove the cores and seeds. Cut a small slice away from the rounded side of each pair to keep it steady when filling and baking. Sprinkle the pears with lemon juice to keep them from turning brown. Arrange the pears core side up in a baking dish.

In a small bowl, toss the blue cheese, dried cherries, and walnuts together and stuff each pear. In the same bowl, whisk together the apple juice, Madeira, and brown sugar until the sugar dissolves. Drizzle the mixture over and around the pears. Bake the pears, basting every 5–10 minutes with the liquid, for 30 minutes or until tender.

Whisk together the olive oil, lemon juice, and ¼ cup of the basting liquid. Toss with the salad mix and divide the greens among 6 plates. Top each salad with a pear half and season with salt and pepper.

Cucumber Tomato Salad

This is a southern classic. Crisp cucumbers, tomatoes, and red on-ions make this salad a go-to on a hot summer afternoon. The key to this salad is letting it get to room temperature so you really taste the fresh produce. This goes well with Green Beans with Fingerling Potatoes (page 53).

MAKES 6 SERVINGS

1 Kirby cucumber, halved lengthwise and thinly sliced
6 medium plum tomatoes, halved lengthwise, seeded, and thinly sliced
¼ red onion, peeled, halved lengthwise, and thinly sliced
3 tablespoons lime-infused olive oil, or more, to taste
1½ tablespoons honey ginger balsamic vinegar, or more, to taste
Coarse salt and black pepper

Toss the cucumbers, tomatoes, and onions in a bowl. In a small bowl, combine the olive oil and balsamic vinegar. Adjust oil and vinegar at this point to your taste. Set aside.

Let the salad rest at room temperature for about 30 minutes. Add the dressing and serve.

Salmon Salad–Stuffed Tomatoes

My mother also made this cool, refreshing salad on hot summer Sundays. We always ate chicken or tuna salad, so salmon salad was a nice change. My mother, like Papa, was always good at presenting dishes in their most attractive packages. This one is stuffed in tomatoes.

MAKES 6 SERVINGS

3 pounds cooked salmon, chilled

2 celery stalks, diced

⅔ cup diced red onions

⅓ cup mayonnaise

2 tablespoons lemon juice

1 tablespoon Capitol Hill Seasoning (a mix of shallots, salt, black pepper, dill weed, parsley, and chives)

6 German Johnson tomatoes (or your favorite heirloom tomatoes)

Salt, to taste

2 tablespoons chopped flat-leaf parsley

Flake the salmon and place it in a large bowl. Add the celery and onions.

In a small bowl, mix the mayonnaise, lemon juice, and seasoning. Set aside for 5–10 minutes to let the flavors meld together.

Combine the salmon and the dressing and refrigerate for at least 2 hours.

When you are ready to serve, rinse the tomatoes. Working with 1 tomato at a time, slice off the top. Using a grapefruit knife, carefully cut around the circumference of the cut side of the tomato all the way around. Gently poke the curved tip of the knife down to the bottom of the tomato, being careful not to pierce the tomato skin. Lift out the soft center and core and discard. Repeat with the remaining tomatoes. Salt the inside of the tomatoes.

Spoon the chilled salmon salad into the tomatoes. Garnish with the parsley and serve.

Gala Apple Chicken Salad

On a hot summer Sundays, my mother often served a cool salad plate for dinner. A good chicken salad served with a Waldorf salad was always a favorite. The two flavor profiles combined in one salad really create a very satisfying main dish.

MAKES 6 SERVINGS

½ cup chopped walnuts
3 cups chopped cooked chicken breast
1 cup seedless red grapes, halved
1 large Gala apple, diced
1 cup diced celery
½ cup mayonnaise, or more, to taste
½ cup slaw dressing, or more, to taste
   (I recommend Marzetti's)
Salt and black pepper, to taste

Preheat the oven to 350°. Bake the walnuts in a single layer in a shallow pan for 6–8 minutes or until toasted, stirring halfway through.

Combine the chicken, grapes, apples, celery, and walnuts in a large bowl. Whisk together the mayonnaise and slaw dressing in a small bowl. Add the dressing to the salad and stir to coat. Season with salt and pepper.

Serve chilled.

Breads

There was nothing like seeing a pan covered by a
tea towel knowing that underneath were homemade
yeast rolls rising for Sunday supper. We didn't have
bread every day of the week but always on church day.
Bread punctuates the meal. I have included recipes here
ranging from Sunday Yeast Rolls to The Pit's Pumpkin
Cornbread Muffins. Don't forget the butter.

Classic New York Challah

Don Mazzia's earliest childhood memories are of bread. A native New Yorker, he grew up in the predominantly Jewish Stuyvesant Town, a project on the Lower East Side of Manhattan built for veterans returning from World War II. Mazzia comes from Italian and Greek-Scot heritage. "The smell of bread baking as we drove through Queens past the Silvercup bakery is a significant childhood memory," he says. "I love that smell." So it is no wonder that when Don studied at the Culinary Institute of America in Hyde Park, New York, one of his favorite courses of study was breads.

Don owned his own specialty wholesale bakery, Triangle Baking Company, in Durham for ten years. He's now the baker for the Levin Jewish Community Center in Durham. He makes and sells challah, a braided yeast bread, as well as babka and bialys at the center for purchase by the public. He was nice enough to share his wonderful challah recipe for families of all faiths.

MAKES 3 MEDIUM-SIZE LOAVES

½ cup canola oil
1½ cups water
5 large eggs, divided
½ cup sugar
2 tablespoons plus 2 teaspoons instant dry yeast
6 cups good-quality bread flour (such as King Arthur)
4¼–4½ teaspoons salt (depending on your preference on salt)
2 tablespoons water

Combine the oil, water, and 4 of the eggs in the bowl of a stand mixer fitted with the dough hook attachment. Add the sugar and the yeast. Turn the mixer on first speed for a minute, allowing it to fully break up the egg yolks. Add the flour and salt and start the mixing process for 2 minutes on first speed. Watch out for initial flour spewing. Turn the mixer to second speed and beat for at least 6 minutes but not more than 10. When fully developed, the dough will pull away from the inside of the bowl. "It should be wet-looking, but smooth and pliable yet strong, which could be described as a silly putty-like gestalt," Don says.

Let the dough rest in the bowl on the table or countertop for at least 5 minutes but not more than 30. Don explains, "After the dough has been jumbled up in the mixer, the gluten strands must relax somewhat for a proper division to take place." Also, while the dough rests, more gluten is developed during fermentation. "You don't want to wait too long on it," Don cautions.

Divide the dough into six equal pieces and shaped into balls. Cover the balls with plastic wrap or a cloth and let rest/rise for about 30 minutes.

Form each piece of dough into a rope approximately 18 inches in length. Take care not to overwork the dough. "The dough can be beaten down and killed at this point," Don cautions. "Don't let this happen. Allow the dough to retain its strength and integrity."

To braid the challah, place 2 of the ropes on your work surface to form an X, laying the first strand angled left to right and the second angled right to left.

To form the loaves, imagine the ends of the bottom strand are labeled A and C and the ends of the top strand, B and D. Lift end A and cross it over the top strand to place it above end C, then lift end C and cross it over to place it where A was. Lift end B and cross it over to place it above end D; lift end D to cross it over to place it where B was. Repeat these 4 steps until the braided loaf is formed, about 6–10 times (depending on the length and thickness of the ropes). The loaf will take form toward you.

At the end of the braiding, pinch the 2 strands together at either end of the loaf with force and tuck them tightly underneath the loaf.

To proof the dough, preheat the oven on the lowest setting for approximately 10 minutes, line a large baking sheet with parchment paper, and spray the paper with cooking spray (expect the dough to double, so make sure the pan is large enough for both loaves to expand without touching).

Place the loaves on the prepared pan and drape a moist kitchen towel over them. (The towel prevents the loaves from drying out during the proofing process but should not be so heavy as to impede the "doubling" of the bread.) Turn off the oven, place the pan inside, and let the bread rest for 30–45 minutes. The surface of the bread will feel tender to the touch when properly proofed (fermented). The challah is very fragile at this stage.

Preheat the oven to 400°. Spray just the corners of the baking sheet with cooking spray to help the parchment lay flat and then spray the parchment paper itself all over.

Mix the remaining egg with the water and brush it on the loaves. The egg wash adds to the aesthetic value, giving the loaf a nice crust and shine. It also helps to keep the braids separate during the baking process. Adjust the egg/water ratio to suit your personal preference.

Place the baking sheet on top of another one; this helps to insulate the pan so the bread won't burn on the bottom.

Put the bread in the oven and reduce the temperature to 350°. Bake for 25–35 minutes.

To test for doneness, with oven mitts, gently pick up a loaf. Pay close attention to how firm it feels. If the braids are sticking together, it's likely done. Tap the underside of the loaf with a sharp flick of your finger; it should sound more hollow than solid.

To cool, remove the loaves from the baking sheet and set on a wire rack.

Serve warm.

NOTE ❊ This freezes well (up to 1 month), but I prefer to use the leftover challah to make French toast for breakfast on Monday.

Sunday Yeast Rolls

My mother told me that when she was growing up, my grandmother made the yeast rolls. She recalled grandma started the bread with a mashed potato.

MAKES 24 ROLLS

2¼ teaspoons active dry yeast

¼ cup warm water

1 cup scalded whole milk, cooled

1 small white potato, peeled, boiled, and run through a potato ricer

¼ cup vegetable shortening

¼ cup sugar

1½ teaspoons salt

4½ cups all-purpose flour

4 tablespoons butter, melted

In a bowl, dissolve the yeast in the water. Let stand until the yeast softens and begins to form a creamy foam, about 5 minutes.

Combine the milk, potatoes, shortening, sugar, and salt in a large bowl. Stir in the yeast. Add 2 cups of the flour and stir until incorporated. Stir in the remaining flour to make the dough.

Turn the dough onto a lightly floured surface and knead until smooth and elastic, about 7 minutes. Place the dough in a lightly oiled bowl, turning the dough to coat it on all sides with oil. Cover the bowl and put in a warm place until the dough has doubled in size, about 1 hour.

Punch down the dough and shape it into a ball. Cover the bowl and let it rest for 10 minutes.

Preheat the oven to 400°. Grease 2 baking sheets.

Shape the dough into 24 rolls and place onto the prepared baking sheets. Let rise for 1 hour. (Grandma was careful to place the baking sheets in an area of the kitchen that wasn't prone to drafts.)

Bake the rolls for 10–12 minutes. Brush the melted butter over the tops and serve.

The Pit's Pumpkin Cornbread Muffins

I still remember the first time I had this moist pumpkin cornbread served with whipped maple butter several years ago at The Pit restaurant in downtown Raleigh, North Carolina. I was struck by the genius of pairing pumpkin purée with cornmeal. This makes for a moist and seasonal cornbread. In fact, it's become so popular that the restaurant now serves it year-round.

MAKES 18 MUFFINS

- $3/4$ cup sugar
- 3 eggs, beaten slightly
- $1\frac{1}{3}$ cups buttermilk
- 1 cup canned pumpkin purée
- $1\frac{1}{3}$ cups white or yellow cornmeal
- $1\frac{1}{3}$ cups all-purpose flour
- $3/4$ teaspoon salt
- $1\frac{1}{2}$ teaspoons baking soda
- $1\frac{1}{2}$ teaspoons baking powder
- $1/8$ teaspoon cinnamon
- Pinch of nutmeg
- $1/2$ cup unsalted butter, melted

Preheat the oven to 350°. Use an all-purpose cooking spray to grease a muffin tin. Set aside.

Mix the sugar, eggs, buttermilk, and pumpkin in a medium bowl until well blended. Set aside.

In a separate bowl, combine the cornmeal, flour, salt, baking soda, baking powder, cinnamon, and nutmeg. Add the wet ingredients to the dry ingredients and mix well. Add the melted butter and stir until thoroughly combined.

Spoon the batter into muffin tin, about ⅔ the way full. Slam muffin tin down on kitchen counter several times to release air bubbles. Bake for 20–25 minutes, turning the pan 180° after the first 10 minutes. The muffins are done when the tops are set and a toothpick inserted into a muffin comes out clean.

NOTE ❊ To make the Pit's whipped maple butter, whip 1 stick of room temperature unsalted butter in a mixer with maple syrup to taste and a pinch of salt.

Stephanie Tyson's
Sweet Potato Biscuits

As a food writer, I get to interview some of North Carolina's best chefs. I had the pleasure of interviewing Chef Stephanie Tyson when her cookbook, Well, Shut My Mouth! The Sweet Potatoes Restaurant Cookbook, was released in 2011. Tyson and Vivián Joiner serve these biscuits and other yam-inspired dishes at their Sweet Potatoes restaurant in Winston-Salem. These biscuits are perfect for stuffing with slices of ham during Sunday dinner.

MAKES 12–18 SERVINGS

2 cups all-purpose flour

¼ teaspoon baking soda

3 teaspoons baking powder

2 tablespoons sugar

¼ teaspoon cinnamon

¼ teaspoon nutmeg

¼ teaspoon ground cloves

½ teaspoon salt

½ cup vegetable shortening, chilled

4 tablespoons unsalted butter, chilled and cubed

¾ cup buttermilk

1 baked medium sweet potato, mashed

Melted butter, to taste

Preheat the oven to 400°. Line a large baking pan with parchment paper.

Sift together the flour, baking soda, baking powder, sugar, cinnamon, nutmeg, cloves, and salt into a medium bowl. Cut in the shortening and butter with a fork until the mixture resembles coarse meal.

In a separate bowl, combine the buttermilk and mashed sweet potato. Add this to the flour mixture, and stir until combined. The dough will be very wet.

Turn the dough onto a well-floured surface and knead just until it starts to come together. Roll the dough to about ½-inch thickness and cut with a 2-inch biscuit cutter; place the biscuits on the prepared pan. For biscuits with soft sides, place them so they are almost touching. Otherwise, place them 2 inches apart.

Bake for 10–12 minutes or until the biscuits are golden brown. Brush with melted butter.

Pumpkin Bread

My dear friend Hillary Hebert of Raleigh, North Carolina, serves this spicy bread every Thanksgiving. She's often blessed me with a couple of loaves as a holiday gift. This moist bread makes a nice companion for Sunday dinner, and certainly a warm slice makes for a wonderful afternoon snack with a hot cup of tea. The recipe comes from her mother, Mary Elizabeth Martin, known affectionately as "Mary Lib." Hillary included this beloved recipe on the back of her mother's funeral program. Hillary recalls that her mother often layered cream cheese between two thin slices of the dessert-like bread, making it even more delicious. This bread freezes well and can be easily thawed overnight for a special breakfast.

MAKES 3 LOAVES

3½ cups all-purpose flour

2 teaspoons baking soda

1½ teaspoons salt

1 teaspoon nutmeg

1 teaspoon cinnamon

4 eggs

⅔ cup water

1 cup canola oil

3 cups sugar

2 cups pumpkin purée

Preheat the oven to 350°. Grease three 8 × 4-inch loaf pans with vegetable shortening.

Sift together the flour, baking soda, salt, nutmeg, and cinnamon into a medium bowl and set aside.

In a separate bowl, beat the eggs well. Add the water, oil, and sugar. Stir half of the flour mixture into the mixing bowl, then add the pumpkin. Add the remaining flour and beat well.

Pour the batter into the pans. Bake for 1 hour. Because the middle of the bread rises quite a bit, Hillary recommends testing with a wood skewer instead of a toothpick to be sure the bread is done all the way through. Allow the loaves to cool for 10 minutes, then turn them onto cooling racks.

NOTE ✳ Mary Lib, a former home economics teacher and prescient recycler, stored her fragrant, spicy loaves in clean plastic newspaper bags.

Irish Soda Bread with Currants and Raisins

Former Vermont Studio Center chef Dorothy Koval of Lake El-more, Vermont, made this delicious Irish Soda Bread several times per week during my one-month fellowship at the retreat for art-ists and writers in April 1998. She packed the bread with lots of raisins, currants, and caraways seeds. While I was working on my writing at the center, I was also fortunate enough to witness her true creativity in the kitchen. I worked in the kitchen to help defray some of my fellowship cost. Dorothy's amazing dishes and breads really fueled our souls as we worked. At the end of my time there, Dorothy shared her Irish Soda Bread recipe with me. You might want to double this recipe to make sure there will be some leftovers for Monday's lunch to accompany a hot cup of home-made soup. Dorothy says this bread also travels well as a snack on a long trip and freezes well.

MAKES 2 MEDIUM OR 3 SMALL LOAVES

2$\frac{1}{2}$ cups all-purpose unbleached flour

2 teaspoons baking powder

1 teaspoon salt

$\frac{1}{2}$ teaspoon baking soda

$\frac{1}{2}$ cup currants

1 cup raisins

1 tablespoon caraway seeds

1 teaspoon decorticated cardamom seeds

4 tablespoons unsalted butter, plus more for brushing tops of loaves

$\frac{1}{2}$ cup sugar, plus more for sprinkling tops of loaves

1 large egg, beaten

1$\frac{1}{2}$ cups full-fat buttermilk

Preheat the oven to 375°. Butter two or three loaf pans (see Note). (You can also shape these on a buttered cookie sheet.)

In a large bowl, sift together the dry ingredients. Combine the raisins, currants and seeds in a separate bowl and toss with a handful of the sifted ingredients so they will not sink in to the bottom of the bread. Set aside.

Using an electric mixer, cream together the butter and sugar. Add the beaten egg and buttermilk until well blended. Don't worry if the buttermilk looks a bit curdled. By hand, fold the wet ingredients into the dry ingredients until moist. Fold in the raisins, currants, caraway seeds.

Fill the prepared pans three-quarters full or shape the dough on the prepared cookie sheet. Drizzle the tops with melted butter and sprinkle liberally with granulated sugar.

Bake for 15 minutes, or until the tops start to brown, then turn the oven down to 325°. Bake until a skewer or small knife inserted into the middle of the loaves comes out clean. The baking time will vary depending on the size of the loaves; the small or the shaped ones will take 30–40 minutes in all; larger ones will take 45–60 minutes. Don't worry about overcooking them. They "will start to smell so good you'll have to check them anyway," Dorothy says.

When cool, turn the bread out onto a baking rack.

NOTE ❋ Dorothy uses two 8½ × 4½ × 2½-inch loaf pans but also says she sometimes multiplies the recipe and puts it into a combination of pan sizes and shapes. Dorothy also notes that these days, it's hard to get anything but low-fat buttermilk, which doesn't have the same qualities as the full-fat version, so she started using half buttermilk and half plain, Greek-style yogurt or sour cream.

Broccoli Cornbread

This is one of the best corn breads I've ever tasted because it's so moist. This recipe comes from the cookbook of Edenton Street United Methodist Church of Raleigh, North Carolina.

MAKES 8–10 SERVINGS

1 cup cooked chopped broccoli, well-drained

4 eggs, beaten

½ cup margarine or butter

6 ounces cottage cheese

1 medium onion, chopped

1 (8.5-ounce) box Jiffy corn muffin mix

1 teaspoon salt

Preheat the oven to 350°. Grease a 9 × 13-inch pan. Combine the eggs, margarine or butter, cottage cheese, onions, corn muffin mix, and salt. Mix well. Stir in the broccoli. Pour the mixture into the prepared pan. Bake for 45 minutes.

Desserts

From cakes to cobblers, any of these decadent sweet treats will end your meal on a high note. My favorites are the Original Baker's German's Sweet Chocolate Cake, the Copper Cricket Amaretto Cheesecake, and, of course, Papa's Nilla Wafer Brown Pound Cake. You will be tempted to eat your dessert first.

Papa's Holiday Hermit Cake

As a child, every Christmas, like clockwork, I could count on two gifts from Papa: a homemade fruitcake and a hermit cake. Papa always made a fruitcake and half a hermit cake for each of his four children and their families.

The hermit cake, which is filled with dates, raisins, English walnuts, and almonds, is believed to have originated as a colonial New England cookie recipe. I'm not sure how the recipe crept into our family tradition, but I'm glad for it.

Papa made the cakes on a weekend afternoon in the fall, often when my mother or aunts could help with the stirring, especially as Papa got older and his hands hurt from arthritis. He baked them in the same fluted pan as his pound cakes. Then he soaked them in his homemade wine, wrapped them tightly in cheesecloth and aluminum foil and let them age for nearly a month.

The cakes arrived at our home sometime between Thanksgiving and Christmas. My mother had her own tradition to greet the arrival of Papa's cakes. She always served the moist slices of hermit and fruitcake to us with hot tea from a real china teapot. My sisters and I sipped the tea from our dainty cups and savored each morsel of hermit cake in our little mouths.

After Papa's death in October 1988, my uncle William Booker became the keeper of Papa's recipe notebook. A few years ago when I visited my uncle's home, he shared with me Papa's most coveted recipes—for his beloved hermit cake and coconut pie.

Papa's instructions for making the hermit cake were incomplete. Even though I am an accomplished cook, I couldn't determine when and how to add the ingredients in a way that would maintain the cake's rich texture. Executive chef Walter Royal of Raleigh's iconic Angus Barn restaurant stepped in and updated Papa's recipe for me. Royal, whose mother also made fruitcakes soaked in homemade wine, said he was impressed with the flavor and moistness of Papa's hermit cake. Royal sent me the cake, and I took it to my mother's home in Lynchburg that Christmas. I saw tears in her eyes. I knew she was thinking about her daddy. Thanks, Walter. You brought back a lot of memories for my family by reproducing this holiday cake.

3 cups unsalted butter, at room temperature

4 cups sugar

9 eggs, separated

7½ cups cake flour, sifted

2½ cups chopped almonds

3½ cups chopped walnuts

2 cups raisins

2 cups chopped dates

3 tablespoons lemon juice

½ teaspoon salt

½ teaspoon baking soda

3 teaspoons baking powder

6 tablespoons cinnamon

3 tablespoons vanilla extract

1 (750-milliliter) bottle fruity white wine

Preheat the oven to 250°. Butter and flour two 10-inch loaf or Bundt pans.

Using an electric mixer, beat the butter and sugar on low speed until a creamy texture is reached, being careful not to overmix. Add the egg yolks one at a time, mixing thoroughly after each addition.

In a separate bowl, whip the egg whites to a firm peak.

In another bowl, combine the flour, almonds, walnuts, raisins, and dates. Fold the butter mixture into the flour mixture. Add the lemon juice, salt, baking soda, baking powder, cinnamon, and vanilla. Fold in the whipped egg whites.

Pour half the batter into each pan and bake for 2¼–2½ hours.

While the cakes are baking, pour the wine into a saucepan and bring it to a boil over medium heat; lower the heat and simmer until the wine is reduced by about two-thirds. When the cakes are done, pour the syrup over the cakes and wrap in cheesecloth. Place in the refrigerator until ready to serve.

Papa's Nilla Wafer Brown Pound Cake

Papa's signature desserts were his pound cake, coconut pie, and hermit cake. Some of the best times I ever shared with Papa were during the execution of these pastries. I loved watching the master at work. Papa cooked with the precision of a chef, carefully measuring his flour with a leftover sugar box. The fragrant perfume of butter and vanilla extract would fill the house. My grandparents' kitchen was below the guest room. That room had a floor grate, so the aroma of food being cooked downstairs rose to the upstairs rooms. When Papa took his pound cake out of the oven and turned it out, he'd inspect its color. "Nilla wafer brown, nilla wafer brown," he'd pronounce. That meant it was a good one.

MAKES 10–12 SERVINGS

1 cup unsalted butter, at room temperature

1 Crisco Butter Flavor All-Vegetable Baking Stick

3 cups sugar

5 medium eggs, at room temperature

2 teaspoons vanilla extract

3 cups cake flour

¼ teaspoon salt

1 (5⅓-ounce) can Carnation sweetened condensed milk

2 ounces water

Prepare a fluted Bundt cake pan by coating the inner surface with the residue from the butter wrapper.

Using an electric mixer, cream the butter, shortening stick, and sugar until fluffy. Crack the eggs into a separate bowl and, with the mixer running, slowly add them into the mixing bowl. Add the vanilla.

Sift together the flour and salt into a separate bowl. Combine the condensed milk and water. Add ⅓ of the flour mixture to the creamed butter mixture and mix well. Add ½ of the milk and water mixture and beat well. Add another ⅓ of the flour mixture, the rest of the milk, and then the rest of the flour mixture, beating well after each addition.

Pour the batter into the prepared pan. Tap the pan on the counter to release the air bubbles.

Place in a cold oven and set it at 325°. Bake for about 1 hour or until a skewer inserted in the middle of the cake comes out clean. Turn the cake out onto a plate. Let it cool before serving.

Peach Cobbler

My friend Lanita Pace-Hinton of Richmond, California, loves good southern food. Her mother, Addie Mae Pace, is originally from Columbia, Mississippi. She picked up tips and tricks from the good cooks she was surrounded by when she moved to New Orleans, Louisiana. This juicy peach cobbler topped with a light and flaky lattice crust offers nuanced spice notes of cinnamon and nutmeg.

MAKES 10–12 SERVINGS

2 boxes Pillsbury refrigerated piecrusts (4 crusts total)

¾ cup butter, cubed

¾ cup all-purpose flour

2 (29-ounce) cans sliced peaches with their juice

6–10 ounces evaporated milk

1 cup sugar

1½ teaspoons cinnamon

1 teaspoon nutmeg

1 teaspoon allspice

2 tablespoons vanilla extract

Preheat the oven to 350°. Line a 9 × 13-inch baking pan with 2 of the piecrusts, trimmed to fit.

Place the butter in a large skillet and heat until it begins to froth in the pan. Sift in the flour, stirring consistently until it becomes a thick paste, tan in color. Slowly pour the peaches and the juice into the butter and flour paste, cooking and stirring until the mixture thickens. Add the evaporated milk as needed to achieve the degree of thickness desired (it should have the weight and consistency of gravy.) Add in sugar and spices, stirring until they are thoroughly incorporated into the mixture.

Pour the peach mixture into the prepared baking dish. Place the remaining piecrusts, trimmed to fit, over the peaches and crimp the edges, or cut the piecrusts into strips and arrange them across the top in a lattice pattern.

Bake for 40 minutes or until the top crust is golden brown. Let cool before serving.

Easy Blackberry Cobbler

My great-aunt Gaynelle Moore of Madison Heights, Virginia, loves making this easy blackberry cobbler for her husband, my great-uncle Melvin, and her Bible study group. She uses the blackberries grown from her own backyard, the homestead of the Moores for more than 100 years now. Uncle Melvin is Papa's youngest brother. Aunt Gaynelle says this recipe is a no-fail one. "You don't have to be rolling the dough; just pour the batter in."

MAKES 6 SERVINGS

2 cups fresh blackberries

2–3 cups sugar, divided

½ cup salted butter

1 cup sugar

1 cup all-purpose flour (see Note)

1 cup evaporated milk

1 tablespoon of baking powder

Preheat the oven to 350°.

Rinse the blackberries and put them in a saucepan. Distribute the sugar evenly over the blackberries and bring to a boil (no need to stir; the berries will make their own juice); reduce the heat and simmer for 10 minutes. Taste the berries to make sure they are sweet enough; if they aren't, gradually add more sugar, to taste. "Blackberries can be kind of twangy," Aunt Gaynelle says, so you may need to add more sugar than you would for other fruits. Remove from the heat and set aside.

Melt the butter in a 2-quart casserole for 5–10 minutes in the oven (but don't let it brown).

In a large bowl, combine the sugar, flour, evaporated milk, and baking powder. Pour the batter into the casserole. Spread the blackberries over the batter. (The batter will rise to the top during baking to create a crust.) Bake for 30–40 minutes or until the crust is golden brown and the filling is bubbly.

Serve warm with your favorite ice cream.

NOTE ❋ You can use self-rising flour here; if you do, omit the baking powder.

Fresh Fall Apple Cake

This was another hit at the potlucks in the features department at the newspaper. Ann Lee's moist, spicy-sweet cake with chunks of tender apples and walnuts is the perfect dessert for a autumn Sunday dinner. This cake's fragrant notes of cinnamon will draw family members and guests to the table. Ann normally served the cake without icing, but I make it a little more decadent for Sunday dinner by adding caramel icing and toasted walnuts.

MAKES 12–15 SERVINGS

FOR THE CAKE

1½ cups sugar

3 eggs

1 cup vegetable oil

2 cups self-rising flour

1 teaspoon vanilla extract

1½ teaspoon cinnamon

¼ teaspoon nutmeg

3 cups finely chopped Gala apples

1 cup walnuts, chopped

FOR THE ICING

1 cup brown sugar

½ cup unsalted butter, at room temperature

5 tablespoons milk

Pinch of salt

1 teaspoon vanilla extract

1 cup powdered sugar

½ cup chopped toasted walnuts (see Note)

Preheat the oven to 350°. Spray a 10-inch Bundt pan with nonstick baking spray with flour.

To prepare the cake, combine the sugar, eggs, and oil in the large bowl of a stand mixer. Beat until blended well, about 1 minute. Add the flour, vanilla, cinnamon, and nutmeg and blend well. Stir in the apples and chopped walnuts.

Pour the batter into the prepared pan and bake for 40–50 minutes or until a knife inserted into the center of the cake comes out clean.

Let the cake cool for at least 30 minutes before turning it out onto a plate. Let it cool for about 1 hour or so before icing.

To prepare the icing, combine the brown sugar, butter, milk, and salt in a medium saucepan over medium-high heat. Bring to a boil and cook, stirring constantly, for 3 minutes.

Remove from the heat and add the vanilla. Beat the icing with a hand mixer on medium speed for about 1 minute. Add the powdered sugar and beat again until smooth.

When the cake is cool, drizzle the icing across the cake with a spoon, allowing it to drip down the sides of the cake; it will pool a bit on the cake plate. Decorate the top of the cake with the toasted nuts.

Serve the cake at room temperature or warm with caramel ice cream. Leftovers are great on Monday morning with a cup of joe.

NOTE ❋ To toast the walnuts, arrange the walnut pieces on a cookie sheet in a single layer and bake in a preheated 350° oven for 8–10 minutes, checking them frequently so as not to burn them. Some ovens, especially over time, run hotter or cooler than the temperature registers. You might want to buy an oven thermometer to get an accurate reading. That way you can increase or decrease the temperature accordingly.

Original Baker's German's Sweet Chocolate Cake

My great-aunt Ellen Harshaw of Silver Spring, Maryland, is known for this buttery, sweet cake. It's labor intensive but worth every minute of the time when you feast your eyes on the three-layer chocolate beauty set off with an icing filled with coconut and pecans. The recipe comes from the label of the Baker's German's Sweet Chocolate Bar, as does the Coconut-Pecan Filling and Frosting recipe that goes with it. Ninety-one-year-old Aunt Ellen, the oldest of Papa's living siblings, made this cake annually for her son Michael's birthday. One year, she made it for mine as well. She hates that she can no longer make the cake for him, but Michael and his wife, Connie, have watched her create it and now make it themselves. So the apprenticeship continues.

MAKES 16 SERVINGS

1 (4-ounce) package Baker's German's Sweet Chocolate
½ cup water
4 eggs, separated
2 cups all-purpose flour
1 teaspoon baking soda
¼ teaspoon salt
1 cup butter, softened
2 cups sugar
1 teaspoon vanilla extract
1 cup buttermilk
Coconut-Pecan Filling and Frosting (recipe follows)

Preheat the oven to 350°.

Cover the bottoms of 3 (9-inch) round pans with waxed paper; spray the sides with cooking spray. Combine the chocolate and water in large microwaveable bowl and heat on high for 1½ to 2 minutes or until the chocolate is almost melted, stirring after 1 minute. Stir until the chocolate is completely melted.

Beat the egg whites in a small bowl with a mixer on high speed until stiff peaks form; set aside. Combine the flour, baking soda, and salt; set aside.

Beat the butter and sugar in large bowl with a mixer until light and fluffy. Add the egg yolks, one at a time, beating well after each addition. Blend in the melted chocolate and vanilla. Add the flour mixture alternately with the buttermilk, beating well after each addition.

Gently fold in the egg whites until well blended. Pour the batter into the prepared pans.

Bake for 30 minutes or until a toothpick inserted in the cake centers comes out clean. Immediately run a small spatula around the cakes in the pans. Cool for 15 minutes; remove the cakes from the pans to wire racks. Cool completely.

Spread the Coconut-Pecan Filling and Frosting between the cake layers and on top of cake.

NOTE ❋ Aunt Ellen says she doesn't use waxed paper, just a nonstick pan and nonstick cooking spray with the flour in it. "It comes out perfect," she declares. She also heats the chocolate in a saucepan on the stove rather than in the microwave and then lets it cool down.

Coconut-Pecan Filling and Frosting

4 egg yolks
1 (12-ounce) can evaporated milk
1$\frac{1}{2}$ teaspoons vanilla extract
1$\frac{1}{2}$ cups sugar
$\frac{3}{4}$ cup butter or margarine
1 (7-ounce) package Baker's Angel Flake Coconut (2$\frac{2}{3}$ cups)
1$\frac{1}{2}$ cups chopped Planters Pecans

Beat the egg yolks, evaporated milk, and vanilla in a large sauce-pan with a whisk until well blended. Add the sugar and butter or margarine; cook on medium heat for 12 minutes or until thick-ened and golden brown, stirring constantly. Remove from heat.

Add the coconut and nuts; mix well. Cool to the desired spreading consistency.

Big Jimmy's Coconut Pie

Papa liked his desserts sweet. This coconut pie is no exception. Enough said.

2 eggs
1 cup sugar
1 tablespoon cornstarch
1½ cups sweetened condensed milk
½ cup unsalted butter, at room temperature
4 ounces shredded unsweetened coconut
1 (9-inch) unbaked pie shell

Preheat the oven to 350°.

In a large bowl, beat the eggs and sugar together. Add the cornstarch, milk, and butter and blend well. Add the coconut and stir until incorporated. Pour the filling into the pie shell. Bake until firm, about 45–50 minutes.

Cool and serve.

NOTE ❋ Add a half teaspoon of vanilla extract to add a little bit more richness. Papa used Jiffy piecrust mix to make his piecrust.

Copper Cricket Café
Amaretto Cheesecake

My first reporting job was in Binghamton, New York, at the Press & Sun-Bulletin. *Far away from home, I was always in search of Sunday dinner. I often ate at the Copper Cricket Café, a small and charming restaurant situated in a house. Rebecca Levy, the salad and pastry chef, noticed one day how many slices I was buying and generously shared the recipe with me. I wrote it down as she recited it from memory. The café has since closed, and Ms. Levy died from breast cancer, but her spirit lives on through the sharing of this recipe. For me, Sunday dinner is all about giving to your friends and family members in the form of a meal. This creamy amaretto cheesecake is always a crowd pleaser, and I always feel loved when I eat it. (Be sure to hide a piece for later. This makes for the most decadent breakfast. But don't tell anybody!)*

MAKES 1 (9-INCH) CHEESECAKE

FOR THE CRUST
1 cup all-purpose flour
¼ cup sugar
½ cup unsalted butter, at room temperature
1 egg yolk
1 teaspoon almond extract

FOR THE FILLING
3 (8-ounce) packages cream cheese, at room temperature
1 cup sugar
4 eggs, at room temperature
1 cup heavy cream
⅓ cup amaretto
1 teaspoon almond extract

¾ cup sour cream
1 tablespoon sugar
1 teaspoon almond extract
Almond slivers, for garnish

Preheat the oven to 375°.

To prepare the crust, mix together the flour and sugar. Cut in the butter until the mixture is crumbly. Add the egg yolk and almond extract and mix well. Press the mixture evenly into the bottom of a 9-inch springform pan.

To prepare the filling, cream together the softened cream cheese and sugar. Beat in the eggs, one at a time, mixing well after each addition. Mix in the heavy cream and amaretto. Add the almond extract and beat the mixture until creamy and smooth (there should be no lumps of cream cheese).

Pour the batter into the prepared pan and bake for 40 minutes.

Meanwhile, prepare the topping: in a small bowl, combine the sour cream, sugar, and almond extract. Spread the mixture evenly over the hot cheesecake. Bake for 5 more minutes.

Run a knife along the inside of the pan and cool the cheesecake on a wire rack for 30 minutes to 1 hour. Refrigerate the cake; when it is completely chilled, remove it from the pan.

Toast the almond slivers on a baking sheet for 10 minutes at 350°. Distribute the almonds over the top of the cheesecake. Serve the cake at room temperature.

Sherbet Cake

On Sundays during the summer when I was a child, a ride after church often meant going to a local ice cream establishment for sherbet. This cool, sweet and tart treat is a light and refreshing dessert on a hot afternoon. No cooking involved, but you need to work quickly to get the tropical layers of sherbet on this yummy cake.

MAKES 8 SERVINGS

---

2 cups whipping cream

3 tablespoons powdered sugar

1 teaspoon vanilla extract

12 macaroon cookies, crumbled

3/4 cup chopped pistachios

2 1/2 cups coconut sherbet, softened

2 1/2 cups mango sherbet, softened

2 1/2 cups raspberry sherbet, softened

Raspberries, for garnish

Chill the whipping cream, a large metal bowl, and the whisk in the freezer for 20 minutes.

Combine the whipping cream, sugar, and vanilla in the chilled bowl. Using the whisk, whip the cream with wide strokes until soft peaks form, switching directions every so often. Fold in the cookie crumbs and pistachios. Spread half of the mixture in the bottom of a 9-inch springform pan and freeze for 30 minutes. Refrigerate the remaining whipped cream mixture.

Using an offset icing knife, spread the coconut sherbet evenly over the whipped cream. Freeze for 20 minutes.

Spread the mango sherbet over the coconut sherbet and freeze for 20 minutes.

Spread the raspberry sherbet over the mango sherbet and then top with the remaining whipped cream mixture.

Freeze for 1 hour or until firm. Thaw for 10 minutes before serving and remove the sides of the pan. Garnish with fresh raspberries and serve.

NOTE ✳ You can use whatever flavors of sherbet or sorbet you like; contrasting colors are nice. When making the whipped cream, the colder the whipping cream, the better. One cup whipping cream yields about 2 cups whipped cream.

Drinks

When I was growing up, a sweet drink was a treat.
There's something refreshing about a pitcher filled
with sweet tea or lemonade or a pretty teapot filled
with a hot, tasty refreshment. These cold and hot drink
recipes, ranging from Palmer Prosecco Punch to Hot
Winter Cranberry Tea, will make your Sunday dinner
guests feel special and pampered.

Iced Peach Tea

Almost everyone loves a cold glass of iced tea, especially in the South. The added flavor of fresh, ripe peaches to black tea gives it an extra lift as a great summer drink.

MAKES 10 SERVINGS

6 regular-size peach-flavored tea bags (see Note)
1 cup sugar
3 cups peach nectar or peach juice drink
1 cup cold water
1–2 tablespoons fresh lemon juice
4 fresh peaches, sliced

Bring 6 cups of water to a boil. Place the tea bags in a pitcher and pour the hot water over them. Brew for 3–5 minutes.

Add the sugar and stir until dissolved. Let the tea cool on the counter for several hours.

Add the peach nectar or peach juice drink and lemon juice and stir. Slice the peaches and add to the pitcher; serve over ice.

NOTE ❋ My personal preference is Stash's Peach Tea. Always allow plenty of time for the tea to cool on the counter before storing in the refrigerator. I like to make tea for Sunday dinner early in the morning, giving it several hours to cool on the counter before placing it in the refrigerator. Sometimes placing the tea in the refrigerator too soon can cause cloudiness. I always use fresh water in my kettle to make tea.

Island Lemonade with Bitters

Hot summer days create a special kind of thirst, one that demands a special kind of lemonade made with fresh lemons, spring water, sugar, ice, and—you won't be disappointed if you try this—a few drops of Angostura bitters. Bitters is an alcoholic beverage flavored with herbal essences like cinnamon, cardamom, anise, and cloves. Imported from the Caribbean nation of Trinidad and Tobago and a favorite of mixologists and cocktail drinkers, Angostura bitters are bitter and tangy and well suited for adding structure and complexity to fruity cocktails. Bitters in this lemonade add a tart flavor that kicks in as soon as the lemon taste recedes from the back of the palate, sending the flavor upward through your nostrils. The end result is a delightful surprise—quenched thirst.

MAKES 6 SERVINGS

---

1 cup sugar

4–5 cups cold water, divided

1 cup lemon juice (about 4–6 lemons), at room temperature (see Note)

3–4 cups cold spring or filtered water (more or less depending on the desired strength)

½ teaspoon Angostura Aromatic Cocktail Bitters

Combine the sugar and 1 cup of the water in a small saucepan over medium heat and stir until the sugar has dissolved completely to make a simple syrup. Combine the simple syrup and the lemon juice in a gallon pitcher. Add the remaining water and the bitters. Refrigerate 1 hour before serving.

If the lemonade is too sweet for your taste, add a little more straight lemon juice to it.

NOTE ✽ When choosing lemons, pick ones that are slightly soft. Avoid the ones that are hard as a rock, as you will have a hard time juicing them.

Hot Winter Cranberry Tea

This hot tea is perfect served for dessert with a tray of an assortment of dried fruits and nuts.

MAKES 6 SERVINGS

7 cups water
6 ounces cranberries (half of a 12-ounce package)
¾ cup sugar
Juice of 1 orange
Juice of 1 lemon
6 whole cloves
1 cinnamon stick

In a large pot, combine the water and cranberries. Bring to a boil, reduce the heat, and simmer for 30 minutes. Add the sugar, orange juice, lemon juice, cloves, and cinnamon stick. Cover, steep for 1 hour, and serve.

Passion Tea with Cranberry Juice

I love combining this blend of hibiscus flowers, herbs, and tropical fruit essences with the crisp taste of light cranberry juice. This is a great drink for family and friends who either are diabetic or don't care for sweet tea.

MAKES 8 SERVINGS

1 (2.85-ounce) filterbag Tazo Iced Passion tea
1 quart chilled Ocean Spray Light Cranberry Juice Cocktail
Thin slices of lime for garnish

Place the tea bag in a 2-quart pitcher. Add 1 quart of boiling water. Steep for 3 minutes and remove the bag. Chill for 1 hour.
Add the cranberry juice and stir well to combine.
Serve over ice and garnish each glass with lime slices.

Cool Cucumber Mint Spa Water

My friend Melanie Wilson of Augusta, Georgia, keeps a pitcher of cucumber spa water on her kitchen counter for gatherings. Her cucumber water refreshes the thirstiest among us on hot days, which can extend deep into October in some parts of the South. She uses flavorful pickling cucumbers or an English cucumber to make this drink as tasty as one with sugar. The drink's appeal is enhanced by using a mason jar; the clear glass shows off the beautiful slices of citrus and cucumbers.

MAKES 8 SERVINGS

1 Kirby pickling cucumber, chilled
1 lemon, at room temperature
3 mint sprigs
Ice
Filtered water

Cut the cucumber into thin slices using a mandolin slicer. Place the cucumber slices in a 2-quart Mason jar. Slice the lemon on the mandolin and add the slices and the leaves from the mint sprigs to the jar. Fill the jar with ice and pour the filtered water over the ice. Cover and refrigerate for at least 2 hours, allowing the flavors to mingle. Serve in pretty, clear glasses.

NOTE ❋ Ice is the key to this calorie-free drink since it keeps the fruit fresh. You can keep adding ice and filtered water all evening. You can also make up your own flavors of spa water by combining other seasonal fruits and herbs.

Prosecco Palmer Punch

This is a bubbly twist on a summer favorite, the Arnold Palmer, a mixture of iced tea and lemonade made famous by the golfer himself. Family members and guests will be sipping on this refreshing sweet and tart drink through dessert. Be prepared to make several pitchers of this sangria-like beverage!

MAKES ABOUT 6 SERVINGS

---

2 bags chai spice tea

$\frac{1}{4}$ cup cane sugar

$\frac{1}{2}$ cup fresh Meyer lemon juice (about 2 lemons)

1 bottle chilled Prosecco

Brew the tea according to the package directions. While the tea is hot, add the sugar.

Let the tea cool on the counter for an hour or so before chilling completely for several hours in the refrigerator. (If you refrigerate the tea too soon, it will turn cloudy.)

Add the lemon juice and pour the tea into a decorative glass pitcher. Add the chilled Prosecco and serve over ice.

Acknowledgments

I would like to thank my mother for answering all my questions about my grandparents and recipes. I appreciate your testing the recipes to make sure I got the details right. Writing is a process, and you need a team. Many thanks to my dear friends who help me birth this book: Andrew Skerritt, for asking probing questions to get to the heart of my feelings about Sunday dinner; Hillary Hebert, for editing recipes and walking with me through the cookbook project; Dana Lindquist Wynne, for edits and feedback; and Kelly Starling Lyons, for testing the recipes.

I was blessed to have been born into a perfect family for a foodie and storyteller. Much love to my aunt Barbara Anne and uncle William Booker and my late uncle Moco for providing me with such wonderful childhood memories at the dinner table and beyond. I'm also grateful to my aunt Shirley and aunt Gaynelle for sharing their input as well.

Some of writing a cookbook is curating great recipes from family, friends, and chefs. I appreciate all of those who shared their recipes and memories with me.

Thanks to Pam Nelson, Mike Richardson, Stephen Miller, Marjorie Hudson, Melanie Wilson, Ann Lee, and Suzanne Brown.

Much gratitude goes to the professionals for sharing their creations: chef Stephanie L. Tyson of Sweet Potatoes Restaurant in Winston-Salem; Samantha Hatem of The Pit restaurant in Durham and Raleigh; Dorothy Koval of Lake Elmore, Vermont, former chef at the Vermont Studio Center; chef Walter Royal of The Angus Barn in Raleigh; and chef Don Mazzia in Durham.

Thanks to fabulous cooks and friends Mary Miller and her husband, Bob Geolas, for all the amazing Sunday dinners at their home and feedback on recipes.

Finally, I owe deep gratitude to my editor, Elaine Maisner, for believing in me and *Sunday Dinner*.

Index